Language in Education
Theory and Practice

Pigeon-Birds and Rhyming Words:
The Role of Parents in
Language Learning

Naomi S. Baron

A Publication of **CAL** Center for Applied Linguistics

Prepared by the **ERIC** Clearinghouse on Languages and Linguistics

PRENTICE HALL REGENTS   Englewood Cliffs, New Jersey 07632

Library of Congress Cataloging-in-Publication Data

Baron, Naomi S.
    Pigeon-birds and rhyming words: the role of parents in language
learning / Naomi S. Baron.
        p. cm. — (Language in education; 75)
    "A publication of Center for Applied Linguistics prepared by the
Clearinghouse on Languages and Linguistics."
    Includes bibliographical references.
    ISBN 0-13-662875-3
    1. Language acquisition—Parent participation.   I. Center for
Applied Linguistics.   II. ERIC Clearinghouse on Languages and
Linguistics.   III. Title.   IV. Series.
P118.B285 1991
401'.93—dc20   90-7527
                                                           CIP

Language in Education: Theory and Practice 75

This publication was prepared with funding from the
Office of Educational Research and Improvement, U.S.
Department of Education, under contract No. RI
88062010. The opinions expressed in this report do not
necessarily reflect the positions or policies of OERI or
ED.

Editorial/production supervision: Shari S. Toron
    Interior design: Whitney Stewart
Cover design: Wanda Lubelska
Manufacturing buyer: Ray Keating

© 1990 by the Center for Applied Linguistics
and by Prentice-Hall Inc.
a Division of Simon & Schuster
Englewood Cliffs, New Jersey 07632

Printed in the United States of America

10 9 8 7 6 5 4 3 2 1

ISBN 0-13-662875-3

Prentice-Hall International (UK) Limited, *London*
Prentice-Hall of Australia Pty. Limited, *Sydney*
Prentice-Hall Canada Inc., *Toronto*
Prentice-Hall Hispanoamericana, S.A., *Mexico*
Prentice-Hall of India Private Limited, *New Delhi*
Prentice-Hall of Japan, Inc., *Tokyo*
Simon & Schuster Asia Pte. Ltd., *Singapore*
Editora Prentice-Hall do Brasil, Ltda., *Rio de Janeiro*

Language in Education: Theory and Practice

ERIC (Educational Resources Information Center) is a nationwide network of information centers, each responsible for a given educational level or field of study. ERIC is supported by the Office of Educational Research and Improvement of the U.S. Department of Education. The basic objective of ERIC is to make current developments in educational research, instruction, and personnel preparation readily accessible to educators and members of related professions.

ERIC/CLL is the ERIC Clearinghouse of Languages and Linguistics, one of the specialized clearinghouses in the ERIC system, and is operated by the Center for Applied Linguistics (CAL). ERIC/CLL is specifically responsible for the collection and dissemination of information on research in languages and linguistics and its application to language teaching and learning.

The ERIC Clearinghouse on Languages and Linguistics (ERIC/CLL) publishes two monographs each year under the series title, *Language in Education: Theory and Practice*. ERIC/CLL commissions specialists to write about current issues in the fields of languages and linguistics. The series includes practical guides, state-of-the-art papers, theoretical reviews, and collected reports. The publications are intended for use by educators, researchers, and others interested in language education.

This publication can be purchased directly from Prentice Hall Regents and will be available from the ERIC Document Reproduction Service, Alexandria, Virginia.

For further information on the ERIC system, ERIC/CLL, and CAL/ Clearinghouse publications, write to Whitney Stewart, Series Editor, ERIC Clearinghouse on Languages and Linguistics, Center for Applied Linguistics, 1118 22nd Street, NW, Washington, DC 20037.

To Ma, whose role is yet to come

Contents

PREFACE   1

Chapter 1
CAN LANGUAGE BE TAUGHT?   5

Chapter 2
LANGUAGE IN CONTEXT   11

Chapter 3
THE BABY TALK QUESTION   18

Chapter 4
THE LANGUAGE DUET: CONVERSATION AND IMITATION   35

Chapter 5
I'D KNOW THAT VOICE ANYWHERE: MODELING SOUNDS   51

Chapter 6
THAT'S A PIGEON-BIRD: THE GROWTH OF MEANING   59

Chapter 7
WOULD YOU LIKE SOME UP?: PARENTS AND GRAMMAR   73

Chapter 8
EXPANDED CONVERSATIONS: READING AND TELEVISION   92

Chapter 9
PROBLEMS ILLUSORY AND ELUSIVE   107

Chapter 10
CONCLUSIONS AND CHALLENGES   117

Preface

This is a book about child language acquisition. Its goal is to examine the role that parents can, do, and should play in the learning process. The book challenges a long-dominant assumption that first language acquisition by children is basically an autonomous affair, in which linguistic input from the surrounding community is largely irrelevant to a biologically determined sequence.

The belief that language learning is essentially independent of environment was a necessary assumption of the Chomskyan school that dominated American linguistics during the late 1960s and throughout the 1970s. According to Chomsky, every newborn comes pre-packaged with a "language acquisition device" that, when combined with some raw data, generates successive models of grammar that drive the growing child's production and comprehension of language (Chomsky, 1965).

I vividly remember explaining this theory to one of my first classes on language acquisition: A group of women in their 30s and 40s—mothers all—who were enrolled in an evening extension program. I was 26 years old and fresh out of graduate school. While I had done extensive research with preschoolers for my dissertation, my knowledge of language acquisition in very young children came largely from books. Halfway through my carefully prepared lecture, one mother of three interrupted: "Does this guy Chomsky have kids? Does he *talk* to them? You know, Prof, Chomsky's got it all wrong."

A howl of approval went up in the classroom. In the face of these veterans' on-the-job experience, my book-learning paled. I knew I would need to rethink what really does go on linguistically between parent and child.

1

Since the early 1970s, a growing number of researchers have taken seriously the question of how parents speak to children. The initial studies of parental "baby talk" (also know as "motherese" or the more non-sexist "child directed speech") were largely empirical analyses of how middle-class American parents address their children. More recent studies have expanded this inquiry to ask whether the ways in which parents speak to children affect their subsequent rate and style of language learning.

Pigeon-Birds and Rhyming Words explores the range of influences parents have upon their children's linguistic development. In the process, it attempts to understand *why* parents adopt the language styles they do in addressing children. The discussion is set in context of three basic themes woven throughout the chapters. The first is the *social* nature of human language that drives parents to adopt a particular style of language with their children. The second is the importance of *multiple variables* in determining the precise effect a specific parent may have upon the language of a particular child. A third theme is the difference between *direct* and *indirect* effects on the learning process.

The focus of the monograph is on the language used by middle-class American parents to their children, but some contrastive remarks are offered about other social and cultural groups. (As we will see in Chapter 2, parental language to children—and styles of parent-child interaction more generally—may vary significantly in different cultural and socioeconomic conditions.) The developmental period covered is from birth through about age 4, because this is the interval during which the essential groundwork for speech—and literacy—is laid down.

Pigeon-Birds and Rhyming Words is divided into ten chapters. Chapters 1 and 2 set the stage—defining the nature-nurture controversy in language acquisition, and identifying variables that help shape linguistic interaction between parent and child. Chapter 3 examines the character and functioning of "baby talk."

The next four chapters (4, 5, 6, and 7) focus on how adults influence their children's development of conversational skills, phonology, lexicon, and grammar, respectively. Chapter 8 turns to parental roles in the development of literacy, and the place of television in language learning. Language problems (real and imagined) are the subject of Chapter 9. Concluding remarks are offered in Chapter 10.

A few notes are in order about my stylistic conventions. I have attempted to balance *he* and *she* when referring to children in the singular. I tend to speak of "parents," and sometimes, specifically of "mothers" when referring to primary caregivers. Obviously, babysitters, relatives, and older siblings play important roles in child rearing, and sometimes the father is the primary caregiver. The choice of "mother" reflects the reality that in contemporary America, child care is largely done by women. What's more, most studies of adult-child linguistic interaction involve mothers, not fathers.

Because this is not a technical book, I have avoided using phonetic notation for utterances that do not follow standard adult pronunciation. (The spellings used instead should make clear the sound combinations being represented.) However, I do make use of the standard linguistic notation for representing a child's age: number of years, followed by a semicolon, followed by number of months (e.g., "2;6" refers to a child who is 2 years and 6 months old).

I have many people to thank for helping to bring this work to fruition. Over the years, members of my language acquisition classes have listened, challenged, and contributed examples and experiences. I am grateful to Whitney Stewart, editor of this series and one of my earliest students, for growing along with me and for inviting me to contribute this monograph. Ursula Schafer kindly provided editorial assistance. My family helped assuage my guilt for all the nights I abandoned hearth and home for keyboard and printer. And finally, I thank Aneil, my son, for offering me the precious opportunity to witness firsthand how parents address children, and what effects parental words can have.

1

Can Language Be Taught?

Noah Webster was renowned for his ability to grasp the precise word appropriate for any circumstance. One day, the story goes, his wife discovered him in bed with a maidservant. "I'm surprised!" Mrs. Webster blurted out. "No, my dear," replied the lexicographer. "I am surprised. You are astonished."

Unlike Webster, many of us tend toward sloppiness in our linguistic choices. We speak of the sun "setting" though we know it is the earth that really moves. We use *shall* or *will, may* or *can, which* or *that* willy-nilly, ignoring the careful distinctions patient school teachers attempted to instill in us years ago.

The subject of this book is children and language, and the role parents play in transforming linguistic neophytes into accomplished language users. To understand the potential influence of adults on this evolving process, we begin by considering the process itself and identifying *le mot juste*—the right word—for describing it.

DEVELOPMENT, ACQUISITION, AND LEARNING

From the moment of conception, human beings undergo continual change. Cells divide, infants begin to crawl, adolescent boys cannot stand girls, graying executives have mid-life crises. As biological organisms, we bear the genetic blueprints for many of our metamorphoses. Yet, as social—and human—creatures, a significant number of our changes are guided by individual initiative and social interaction. Infants learn to crawl only after much trial and error, and children learn to sing only by hearing others carry a tune.

How much of human metamorphosis is biologically determined and how much results from personal action or interaction? The age-old "nature-nurture" controversy is as heated in linguistics as it has been in social or cognitive psychology. Do children *develop* language through biological destiny (much as seedlings develop into saplings)? Do children *acquire* language by letting loose their biological endowment upon the empirical linguistic landscape (like a painter from the Baroque creating a still life)? Or, is language *learned*, with children profiting from the tutelage (conscious or otherwise) of more fluent speakers?

Readers conversant with the linguistic literature will recall the Chomsky-Skinner "debate" between the creator of generative-transformational grammar and the leading exponent of behavioral psychology. B.F. Skinner maintained that human language results from conditioning organisms (here, the human child) to respond appropriately to stimuli (Skinner, 1957). For Skinner, human language is entirely a *learned* skill, nurtured by fluent adults.

Noam Chomsky countered that language is a biological ability unique to *homo sapiens*. Children come into this world as junior grammarians, equipped with neural templates ("language acquisition devices") enabling them to sort through the empirical detritus of everyday language and extract linguistic competence (Chomsky, 1959, 1965). For Chomsky, the emergence of language is a cross between automatically generated biological *development* and an individually *acquired* ability resulting from the growing child actively testing theories against the data at hand.

In recent years, several new groups of players have entered the debate. On the one hand, cognitive psychologists (*née* "psycholinguists") see language as but one among many mental structures that naturally evolve as a child matures—language *development* or *acquisition*. On the other hand, anthropologists and sociologists contribute ethnographic and small group dynamics perspectives, wherein language is a social skill emerging from interaction among members of a group—language *learning*.

Like many theoretical debates, the nature-nurture controversy is reminiscent of the proverbial ten blind men and the elephant; each man apprehending only part of the beast's physique. Language experts in search of a theory of mind emphasize the universal and non-interactive side of language. Those concerned with social dynamics are more prone to discover the role of pedagogy in the emergence of language.

So which is it: development, acquisition, or learning? It is, of course, all three. For unlike the elephant, whose morphology is one and the same for all members of the species, the human child embarking upon his or her linguistic journey is a unique individual living under singular circumstances. The uses that growing children make of their environment are varied and elusive. Just as no two fingerprints are identical, no two children become linguistic via precisely the same path. As outside observers, adults can rarely be certain whether a child's new word or nascent ability to use plurals correctly has resulted from silent observation and analysis, spontaneous imitation, or actual teaching.

In this book, we will talk about language *development*, language *acquisition*, and language *learning*, using the terms roughly synonymously. While Mr. Webster might not approve, the decision helps alleviate the stylistic boredom of more neutral terms like *emergence* or *change*, and prods us into exploring the questions motivating this book: What do parents do, what should they do, and what behaviors should they avoid as their children develop/acquire/learn language?

PARENTS AS PEDAGOGUES: TEACHING AND LEARNING

In the heyday of transformational grammar (roughly 1965-1975), it was commonplace to find studies of language acquisition asserting that first languages are never taught. The main pieces of evidence underlying this claim were first, that children come up with novel words and phrases they could not possibly have learned from others, and second, that parents do not correct their children's linguistic mistakes.

The Novelty Issue

Most of us who have spent time around toddlers or preschoolers have heard children using non-standard terms for things or actions. Many children overgeneralize morphological markers, creating *mans* for *men* or *goed* for *went*. Until he was aged 2, my son Aneil's name for "stairs" was *two* (deriving from our practice of counting the risers each time we ascended or descended the stairs). At age 2;8, the same child coined the term *allbody* (as in, "Good night, allbody"). Because standard English contains neither *mans* nor *allbody*, linguists have rightly taken such lexical and grammatical neologisms as evidence of a creative component to language acquisition.

The Correction Issue

In a landmark longitudinal study of three children, code-named Adam, Eve, and Sarah, Roger Brown and his colleagues at Harvard investigated the early syntactic stages of first language acquisition. One of the parameters analyzed was how adults respond to children's mistakes.

Drawing upon his collaborative work with Camille Hanlon (Brown & Hanlon, 1970), Brown argued that while parents sometimes correct children's pronunciation or morphological overgeneralizations, they do not correct ungrammatical syntax.

> [P]arents seemed to pay no attention to bad syntax nor did they even seem to be aware of it. They approved or disapproved an utterance usually on the grounds of the truth value of the proposition which the parents supposed the child intended to assert. This is a surprising outcome to most middle-class parents, since they are generally under the impression that they correct the child's speech. From inquiry and observation I find that what parents generally correct is pronunciation, "naughty" words, and regularized irregular allomorphs like *digged* or *goed*. . . . But syntax—the child saying, for instance, "Why the dog won't eat?" instead of "Why won't the dog eat?" seems to be automatically set right in the parent's mind, with the mistake never registering as such. (Brown, 1973, p. 412)

Taken together, evidence of linguistic novelty along with Brown's analysis of parental corrections (for syntax, Brown concludes that corrections do not exist) have led many students of language acquisition to conclude that first language is never taught. This conclusion, like rumors of Mark Twain's premature demise, turns out to be greatly exaggerated.

Modes of Teaching, Modes of Learning

None of us is surprised when a child born in Lisbon begins

speaking Portuguese or a toddler from South Boston sounds like a native of Massachusetts, not Montana. How do children know which dialect (or language) to learn? By hearing adults model language.

So much of what we learn comes not through overt pedagogy but by seeing others engage in the behavior. When a 2-year-old climbs into the front seat of the family car, wiggles his hand in the vicinity of the ignition, kicks his feet, and then grabs the steering wheel, he is demonstrating that he has "learned" to drive the car. It is highly unlikely that his parents consciously "taught" the boy these procedures. But what they did do, time and again, was model the sequence of steps involved in getting the car to move.

We present language by being ourselves—by talking with other adults as we move through the day. Sometimes the modeling comes from the language addressed to us. One of my son's playmates in nursery school recently chirped to her mother, "Have a nice day." The woman was surprised because she eschewed the phrase in her own language. Her daughter had probably picked it up from other adults she had encountered—grocery check-out clerks, department store sales people, bank tellers.

Another critical source of modeling is the language we use in conversation with children. While Brown is right that most parents do not play school marm (or master) when their child says "Why the dog won't eat?", parents achieve the same pedagogical effect when they follow up grammatical errors with repetitions, recastings, or continuations of the same topic ("Why won't the dog eat? I guess because he isn't hungry"). As we will see in later chapters, these conversational devices are frequent, typically unconscious, and pedagogically highly effective.

The impact of adult language behavior on children comes through not only in the child's emerging dialect, knowledge of specific words or phrases ("Have a nice day"), or improved grammatical usage. It can also be seen in more subtle forms such as frequency of word usage (see Chapter 6) and even choice of conversational topic.

Many toddlers go through a stage of marching about the house, naming things as they pass: *light, book, table.* Linguists often speak of a "naming explosion" that occurs in the language of children around age two years. When my son began proclaiming names for common household objects, I was initially perplexed. These were not objects over which he paused. He simply labeled them and moved on. Was language learning really, as Bloomfield (1933) and Skinner (1957) had implied, a matter of stimulus (e.g., a book on the floor) automatically, necessarily generating a response, "book"? Suddenly the explanation became clear. The child was not responding to a visual stimulus like a Skinnerian pigeon. Rather, he was mirroring my own behavior as I moved through the day with him: "Look Aneil, that's a light," "Oh, there's a book on the floor. A book, Aneil," or "That's a table. Can you say *table*?"

"That's a table." Not only was I modeling conversation. I was, in fact, teaching. If you listen carefully to parents, you will find them using more overt pedagogy than standard treatises on language acquisition suggest occurs. Admittedly, you should hardly expect to observe parents (even linguist parents) lecturing 4-year-olds on differences between active and passive voice. But, you will find much lexical training ("An iguana is sort of a cross between an alligator and a snake"), a solid dose of overt conversational pedagogy ("It's not your turn to talk yet. Wait until Joannie is finished"), and some pointers on stylistic and logical conventions ("The punch line is supposed to come at the end of the joke—not in the middle").

As any good teacher knows, successful pedagogy is the product not only of sound methodology but of a clear understanding of the learning context. What is the cultural milieu? What is the child's personality like? What other commitments do you, the "teacher," have on your time? What presuppositions do you have about how the learning process should go? In considering the role of parents in children's language learning, it is especially important to place the learners—and their teachers—in context.

2

Language in Context

Those of us watching American television in the 1950s (or reruns of "Leave It to Beaver" or "Father Knows Best" in the 1980s) came away with a strange view of American life. Everyone is middle-class. Women stay home to raise children and serve on the PTA, while fathers go off to unspecified jobs, returning to arbitrate the day's squabbles. No one is divorced, no one seriously ill, and no one has problems that take more than half an hour to resolve.

Language acquisition literature from the 1960s and early 1970s offered a comparably skewed view of reality. Led by both Chomskyan and Piagetian quests for universals, researchers sought commonalties in the ways children within the same community or around the world learn language (e.g., Slobin, 1973). Because all observations are theory-laden (Hanson, 1958), it is hardly surprising that data rolled in confirming language acquisition as a homogeneous, predictable affair.

In the last 15 years, linguists have become increasingly aware that not all children learn language the same way. In this chapter, we will identify the major social and individual variables underlying this variation. Our ethnographic and psychological tour has three stops: cultural customs, family circumstances, and child-centered issues. Information on *how* these variables affect the learning of specific language components appears in the chapters that follow.

CULTURAL CUSTOMS

A society's views on language acquisition often reflect its attitudes toward childhood itself. A welter of studies (e.g., Ariès, 1962; de Mause, 1975; Pollock, 1983; Triandis & Heron, 1981; Leiderman,

Tulkin, & Rosenfeld, 1977) have shown that human societies at different points in space and time vary in their notions of what it means to be a child. Is a toddler a miniature adult? Is childhood a separate period of life during which children are given special consideration in food, clothing, and nurturing? Do we see children as having "incomplete" mental capacities (taking adult abilities as the norm), or do we believe children pass through developmental stages, unique to childhood?

Our assumptions about what kind of people children are color the ways in which we interact with them. The Mohave Indians, for example, believe that fetuses nearing birth are rational and can understand verbal admonitions (Devereux, 1949). If, however, we agree with Immanuel Kant that children are not yet human, it makes little sense to try reasoning with them. If children are blank slates upon which to write, then parents play an important pedagogical role from the start. If we assume children begin with restricted powers of comprehension, we initially modulate the language and information we direct to them.

The ways in which we interact with children are also linked to social assumptions and practices regarding child rearing. Are young children typically cared for by their mothers? by older siblings? by servants? Do fathers take an active parenting role with infants and toddlers?

Such cultural assumptions and practices influence the ways in which we interact with our children linguistically (see Pye, 1986). Should babies be encouraged to vocalize or to keep silent when in the presence of other adults? Is a child's opinion solicited or are decisions made for her? How important is it for children to have diverse social experiences to talk about?

Another cultural issue is the number (and status) of languages and dialects in the community. Are children expected to become bilingual? If so, does the process begin at birth or is it postponed until formal schooling begins? What social standings do the two (or more) languages have in the community? Will the children learn one dialect at home and another at school? Do all members of the society become multilingual (or multidialectal), or is the acquisition of more than one system a class marker?

What are the society's attitudes about the relative status of men and women? In many traditional societies, male children have been more prized than females. The effects of these attitudes may be reflected in child rearing practices. Greece is a contemporary example. A study by Roe, Drivas, Karagellis, and Roe (1985) has pointed up that male infants in Greece vocalize significantly more than do females—the opposite of findings for American infants (e.g., Lewis, 1969; Lewis & Freedle, 1973). Roe et al. suggest that the higher incidence of male vocalization in Greece is in direct response to preferential attitudes and behaviors of Greek mothers toward infant boys.

FAMILY CIRCUMSTANCES

While influenced by cultural patterns of the larger society, the family unit defines the fundamental context in which early language learning takes place. Variety in family circumstances—we are not all the mythical Cleavers of the 1950s—defines markedly distinct learning environments for children. To control or compensate for any of these factors, we must first learn to identify them.

Who belongs to the household: one parent or two? grandparents or other relatives? a full-time or live-in housekeeper or babysitter? How much education do members of the household have?

How old are the parents when the first child is born? A mother of 40 may well have different expectations about how to address a newborn—and what to expect in return—than a mother of 20. Education and parental age often go hand-in-hand. First-time mothers of 40 typically have higher educational credentials than counterparts half their age.

Are there other children in the household? If so, how many years separate them? (The linguistic effect of a 3-year-old sister upon a 2-year-old is fundamentally different from that of a 13-year-old upon a toddler.) Is the child a twin? Does she have other regular playmates her own age (e.g., cousins, neighbors)?

The rhythm of life within the family can also alter the course of language acquisition. Consider possible traumas in a young child's life: the birth of a sibling, moving to a new home, the serious illness or death of a family member, divorce. It is not uncommon for normally developing 2- or 3-year-olds to begin stuttering or even stop speaking for a period of time when such events occur (often along with loss of appetite, incontinence, insomnia, moodiness, or aggression).

What is the ambiance of the household? Quiet or noisy? Does the sound come from conversation? music? television? Does the family eat meals together and, if so, does conversation include more than "Pass the potatoes" or "Don't chew with your mouth full"?

On the subject of television, how many hours a day is it on? Do members of the family actually watch the screen, or do programs serve as background accompaniment for other activities?

What language is spoken in the home? Do the parents have the same native language? If not, are both fluent in a common tongue? Are the parents at ease in using the language of the surrounding neighborhood? If not, what is the parents' socioeconomic standing, and what is the status of their native language in the eyes of the community?

Who generally takes care of the child? In the United States, mothers bear overwhelming responsibility for child rearing. In the chapters that follow, nearly all of the studies cited are based on mother-child interaction. The handful of studies involving language of fathers to children generally compare maternal with paternal speech patterns rather than asking how fathers' speech influences child language development.

The whole issue of how fathers speak to young children is inseparable from the larger question of how much time fathers actually spend with their children and, derivatively, how the amount of contact time influences fathers' beliefs about their children's developing skills. An Israeli study (Ninio & Rinott, 1988) found that the more fathers were involved in the care of their 9-month-old infants, the more cognitively competent those fathers judged their infants to be. How do amount of contact time and resultant perceptions of cognitive ability shape fathers' speech styles to young children? Such questions are very much in need of research. Intuitively, we would expect that the more contact fathers have with their offspring, the more their speech patterns (and expectations) will resemble those of mothers (but see Chapters 4 and 7).

In conducting such studies, it will be very important to distinguish between the amount of time fathers are "around" their children and actual time spent interacting. Ninio and Rinott, for example, report that although fathers in their study were "available" to their 9-month-olds an average of 2.75 hours per day, only 45-50 minutes of that time was spent in actual parenting. Nearly 50% of the fathers in the study never took exclusive responsibility for their babies during waking hours for more than an hour at a time (measured over a period of 10 days). In fact, the average amount of time fathers spent alone with their infants was 8.8 minutes per day. Such data call into question the validity of existing studies (e.g., Hummel, 1982) that distinguish between speech patterns of "high-time-involvement" and "low-time-involvement" fathers on the basis of how many hours fathers are "around" their children, instead of how much real interaction is taking place.

But, are mothers themselves the primary source of language input to their children? In 1960, only 19% of American women with children below the age of 6 were employed (Barnett & Baruch, 1978). Now that 56% of women with children under age 6 are employed (U.S. Department of Labor, 1989), the primary caregiver is often not the mother. A major dilemma for today's parents—from welfare mothers in job training programs to physician parents—is the care of young children. Depending upon the age of the child, family affluence, and the parents' educational philosophy, several strategies are available, including full-time care in the home, group care with a neighbor, or formal day care or nursery programs. Each solution brings with it characteristic patterns of language modeling.

Full-time home care is often selected to emulate the one-to-one relationship (or, with siblings, the one-to-few relationship) between mother and offspring. Sometimes the emulation works—or even surpasses expectations, especially in the case of experienced caregivers. Other times, the amount or style of linguistic interaction is not what we bargained for. An increasing number of housekeepers in America know little or no English. Frequently, the dynamics work well, and the child even grows up bilingual. Yet, in many instances, the result is a linguistic vacuum, with the caretaker initiating very little linguistic exchange. Friendly cooing sounds or tickling routines are useful with infants, but they hardly compensate for the rich verbal patter characteristic of typical mother-child exchanges.

Care outside of the home (with neighbors or in a formal program) brings the advantage of playmates but a potential reduction in the amount of language the adult caregiver can address to individual children. Is group care—and formal day care in particular—detrimental to linguistic development?

A comprehensive review of the effects of day care (Belsky & Steinberg, 1978) reported that "experience in high-quality, center-based day care ... has neither salutary nor deleterious effects upon the intellectual development of the child" (p. 929). However, it is hardly the case that all day care is "high-quality." McCartney (1984), for example, reports from her study of day care in Bermuda that the quality of the day care environment profoundly affects language development. Children benefited linguistically when caregivers used representational language (i.e., giving and requesting of information), whereas children were disadvantaged by the controlling language from caregivers. McCartney also found that the more language that was directed to children by the caregiver (as opposed to by peers), the greater the children's linguistic development.

How do day care (or nursery) programs compare with home-care in the amount of language directed by adults to children? Intuitively, we might assume that children in day care come out the losers (also see Cochran, 1977). Yet, reality is more complex. Teachers in high-quality day care programs and nursery schools spend an enormous amount of time speaking with children (often using more sophisticated language than do mothers), while housewives or housekeepers often park their kids in front of the television or with older siblings. Moreover, as a recent study (Ackerman-Ross & Khanna, 1989) indicates, middle-class parents whose children attend high-quality day care and nursery programs tend to "compensate" in the evenings and on weekends by engaging in concentrated amounts of conversation with their offspring.

The role of nursery programs is further complicated by the increasing amount of pedagogy often going on in the home. Thanks to *Sesame Street*, many American children know their basic numbers and letters by age 2 or 3, and a large number of 4-year-olds who can read are still probably being sent to kindergarten reading readiness classes.

CHILD-CENTERED VARIABLES

However important cultural and family context may be to the language acquisition process, we cannot ignore the most important variable of all: the child himself or herself. Much as a single perfume smells different on different people, the same external influences often yield diverse effects on children growing up under similar circumstances.

Differences in children's temperament and personality surface very early in life (Thomas & Chess, 1977; Buss & Plomin, 1984). By the time they are a few weeks old, most infants have established their own sleeping and eating habits. Within the first few months of life, we can discern differential patterns of learning and of social interaction—inquisitive versus cautious, aggressive versus shy. These personality traits are often echoed in language acquisition patterns. A toddler who is very careful climbing steps may show comparable caution in using only words with phonemes he can articulate and in avoiding words he has difficulty pronouncing. An imaginative child may pick up words like *imagine, remember,* and *pretend* long before more literal age-mates in similar linguistic circumstances.

In evaluating the child's contribution to the language acquisition process, we need to remember how easily we confuse our own perceptions of children (and our presuppositions about appropriate language for addressing them) with the needs and capacities of the children themselves. American parents tend to vocalize more to girl babies than to boys, speak differently to second-born children than to first, and hesitate to interact freely with children they perceive to be abnormal. Distinguishing between the child's and the parent's contribution to the emerging linguistic exchange can become extremely difficult.

The course of a child's language development is an involved product of biological inheritance, individual personality, and influence of external circumstances. The external circumstance to which we now turn is the language parents use in addressing young children.

3

The Baby Talk Question

Ask the average person what role parents play in their children's language learning, and you are likely to get one of two responses. You might hear that parents are irrelevant to the process: Somehow kids manage to pick up language on their own. Alternatively, the respondent might say that parents talk to young children in special ways (like saying *choo choo* for *train* or *doggie* for *dog*), and maybe these modifications speed language acquisition.

Such "special language" is generally known as *baby talk* (i.e., that language appropriate to use when addressing babies). Why do parents use it? Do they use it consistently? Do some parents never use it at all? What effect *does* baby talk have on language learning? And what, if anything, should parents do to encourage or minimize its use? These are the questions we will pursue in this chapter. In the following four chapters, we will look in more detail at the forms, functions, and effects of baby talk on the acquisition of conversational abilities (Chapter 4), sound patterns (Chapter 5), meaning (Chapter 6), and grammar (Chapter 7).

Baby talk arises out of normal conversational give-and-take between adult and child. To understand why baby talk exists and what alternative forms it assumes, we best begin with broader questions concerning conversation and language function.

THE ART OF CONVERSATION

To state that conversation lies at the heart of human language is not to say that we use language only to exchange pleasantries or gossip. Far from it. Human language has a wide range of functions: to inform, to harangue, to plead, to jest, to teach, and more. In fact, we often use a single sentence to accomplish several jobs at once. When a mother says to her 3-year-old, "Do you think it's time to put away your trucks and go to bed?", she is simultaneously

(1) asking a question (Do you really think it's time?),

(2) making a request (How about doing it now?), and

(3) teaching (Before children go to bed, they need to pick up their toys).

Language Functions

The uses of human language are rich and varied. A number of linguists (including Bühler, 1934; Jakobson, 1960; Baron, 1981) have charted the spectrum of human language functions. Jakobson, whose schema is best known, identifies six distinct types of functions language may serve.

referential (conveying information)

emotive (indicating the feelings of the speaker)

conative (expressing the speaker's feelings about the addressee)

poetic (focusing on the style of the message itself)

phatic (using language to keep the lines of communication open)

metalingual (employing language to talk about language)

Given our interest in language acquisition, we will address the question of language function somewhat differently. Our goal here is to understand the ways in which adult speech can affect the language of children. Therefore, we need to focus on how language functions in human *interactive* behavior.

Language-as-interaction is divisible into five main areas.

pedagogy

control

affection

social exchange

information

The *pedagogical* function is self-explanatory: using language to teach (e.g., "An iguana is sort of a cross between a lizard and an alligator" or "Don't talk with your mouth full"). We use language in a *controlling* function when we try to get someone's attention ("Stop that!" or "Look over here"). Language expresses *affection* when we whisper sweet nothings in our loved one's ear or say "Would Ralphie like his milkbone?" to our pet poodle.

By *social exchange*, we refer to the same domain as Jakobson's phatic function: using language to keep social communication going. Finally, *information* is what is left over when we have parceled out the other functions. Because so much of what we say has multiple functions, the information function is almost always coupled with another purpose—most typically, social exchange. When I tell you how I spent my summer vacation, I am at once informative and social. Another common pairing of functions is the informative with the pedagogical (e.g., when giving directions from the airport to your house). About the only time language functions purely informationally is in response to pragmatic questions ("Is this Peachtree Plaza?" "Yes").

The Issue of Style

The conversational richness of human language derives not only from the range of functions it fills, but from the linguistic styles (or *registers*) we use to fill them. Depending both upon the social uses to which we are putting language and upon who we are (e.g., male or female, young or old, high or low in social status), we settle upon one of many possible speech registers. We address the maître d' at *The Four Seasons* differently than we do the check-out clerk at the grocery store or the IRS agent auditing our tax return. In fact, not only do we speak differently to the *staff* at *The Four Seasons* ("This evening, I believe we might try the Chateaubriand") than to their counterparts at the local deli ("Gimme a hot pastrami"), but our conversational tone with our dining companions often "dresses up" or "dresses down" to fit the decor and the bill.

As speakers of English, we each develop *communicative competence* (Hymes, 1974) in the language—knowing when to say what to whom. Children acquire these rules of talk at the same time they are gaining command over sounds, grammar, and vocabulary.

In addition to conscious modeling of different speech registers to teach our progeny (e.g., religiously saying "Thank you" each time an object is passed to us), we also use these styles in the normal course of conversation with our children. Especially with younger children, we sometimes adopt the special speech style known as *baby talk*.

BABY TALK: WHAT IS IT?

The linguistic literature and popular lore are filled with references to *baby talk* (or *motherese,* or the more neutral term *child directed speech*). All of these labels refer to a set of speech traits commonly found in the language adults use to address young children, especially between birth and about age 4. Some of the early literature (e.g., Ferguson, 1964) reported that similar traits are found in adult speech to children in vastly different societies around the world. In fact, some linguists (e.g., Lewis, 1957) have spoken of baby talk as a universal feature of adult speech to young children.

When linguists refer to baby talk, they usually have in mind an adult-to-child speech style that differs from typical adult-to-adult speech in its sound patterns, word choice, and syntactic and conversational style. Figure 3.1 presents a summary profile of this special speaking style.

PHONOLOGICAL FEATURES
higher pitch
greater range of frequencies
slower rate of speech
clearer enunciation
emphasis on one or two words in a sentence
special pronunciation of individual words

LEXICAL FEATURES
substitutions
diminutives
semantically inappropriate words
use of child's nonce forms

SYNTACTIC FEATURES
use of nouns in lieu of pronouns
use of plural pronouns in place of singular
intentional ungrammatical usage
more grammatically correct usage
more grammatically simple phrases
shorter phrases

CONVERSATIONAL FEATURES
more restricted topics
more repetitions of own utterances
more questions, fewer declaratives
more deictic declaratives
provision of both questions and answers by adult
repetitions, expansions, recasts of child's utterances

Figure 3.1   Profile of Common Baby Talk Features

Let us be sure we understand to which dimension of baby talk each of these features refers.

Phonological Features

The phonological dimension of baby talk is the easiest to recognize. Especially when addressing infants, parents often combine heightened fundamental frequency (i.e., pitch) and greater than normal modulation of pitch across the utterance. Baby talk addressed to toddlers also tends to have its own phonological profile. Adult speech here is often slower in pace and more clearly enunciated. In addition, many parents find themselves placing special emphasis on one or two words in a sentence (e.g., "So that's a *dinosaur*, is it?") or lending a unique pronunciation to a word (e.g., "Do you have a *li-i-tle* hurt on your finger?").

Lexical Features

The most common lexical features of baby talk are substitutions (e.g., *tum-tum* instead of *stomach*) and diminutives (e.g., *doggie* for *dog*). Other lexical adjustments include the use of semantically inappropriate words (e.g., intentionally calling a whale a *fish*) or incorporation of a child's original word into one's own language (e.g., following my son between the ages of 1;6 and 2;6, I took to calling an airplane a *go*).

Syntactic Features

Two syntactic features of baby talk are especially common: use of nouns in lieu of pronouns ("Mommy wants Sarah to drink her milk") and use of plural pronouns in place of singular ("Do we want to go to bed now?"). A third feature of baby talk, intentional use of an ungrammatical construction (e.g., "Would you like some up?" meaning "Do you want to be picked up?") is also distinctive. However, several other features that are clustered (notably, using sentences that are more grammatically correct, grammatically simpler, and shorter than typically found in adult-to-adult speech) do not strike us as linguistically special until we explicitly compare them with the normal speech we use in addressing adults.

Conversational Features

Like the last three syntactic features, conversational features of baby talk stand out only in retrospect when we analyze transcriptions of adult-child conversations. Yet, their elusive character in no way diminishes their importance.

Conversationally, baby talk tends to be very limited in scope: The range of topics is restricted, not only by the subjects, but by the fact that parents repeat what they say ("Would you like some juice? Would you like some juice?"). Structurally, the parent's end of the conversation is heavy on questions and short on declaratives (the exception being the deictic declarative, e.g., "That's a ball"). In fact, especially with children under age 2, parents often supply both the question and the answer ("Shall we go outside now? Yes. That's a good idea").

The least easily recognized—and probably the most important—conversational feature of baby talk is the use of sentences based upon children's previous utterances. These adult responses assume several forms: direct repetition of what the child has said (often for the purpose of checking that we understood correctly), expansion of the child's utterance (e.g., Child: "Water off"; Adult: "Yes, let's turn the water off now"), and recasts that use the child's previous utterance to further the conversation (e.g., Child: "Water off"; Adult: "But, if we turn the water off, we won't be able to wash our hands").

WHY BABY TALK?

Why do these manifestations of baby talk tend to co-occur, at least in the speech of contemporary middle-class American parents? Do baby talk features have some internal coherence, or are they accidental bedfellows, like items scribbled on a shopping list?

That which binds together the notion of baby talk is less a special set of language features than a *state of mind* that is *manifested* in diverse linguistic ways—some ways are expressed through special language forms, but others become distinctive only in the consistency of their patterning.

The full constellation of baby talk features is by no means universal (see, for example, Ochs, 1982; Pye, 1986). In fact, even within a single culture such as contemporary middle-class America, parents differ sharply in their use of the features listed in Figure 3.1. To understand the sources of baby talk variation across speakers and to comprehend why the baby talk profile itself is such a hodgepodge, we need to think about the following sorts of questions regarding language function.

Why do we address people the way we do?

Are the ways in which we speak to children similar to our speech styles with adults?

If so, do similar forms express similar functions?

Where do special language forms, such as baby talk, come from?

Let us return, then, to the five basic language functions we identified—*pedagogy, control, affection, social exchange,* and *information*. As we will see, the same functional motivations underlying adult speech to children also motivate adult speech to other adults as well. That is, adult-to-child speech is part of the larger framework of conversation we have with fluent members of a speech community. Therefore, we will need to examine the ways these functions drive *both* the speech that adults address to young children, *and* the speech that adults address to other adults. Our goal is a clear picture of the reasons baby talk exists (when it does), the reasons its use and forms are so varied, and the reasons it is sometimes structurally indistinguishable from language used for similar purposes when addressing interlocutors other than children.

WHY BABY TALK? A CAUSAL VIEW

Figure 3.2 offers a visual summary of the five interpersonal language functions that adults use when they speak with others (be they children or other adults).

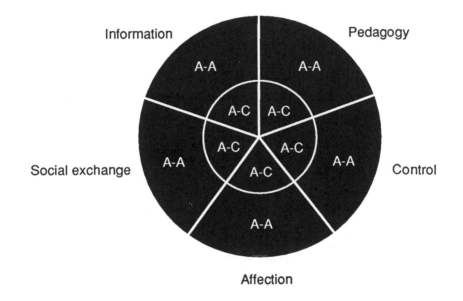

A-A Adult-to-adult utterance
A-C Adult-to-child utterance

**Figure 3.2 Functions of Adult Speech to Adults
and to Children**

We will look, in turn, at each of the five functions, examining the kinds of "special language" that emerge in adult speech. In each case, we will first consider the language adults address to young children, and then turn to adult speech intended for other adults.

Throughout our analysis, we must be mindful of two caveats. First, a "special language" feature may be generated by more than one functional motivation. Second, the very attempt to identify a speaker's motivations can be a precarious undertaking. The same sentence uttered by two speakers under identical external circumstances may stem from divergent motivations.

Consequently, the functional categorizations offered below represent plausible—not definitive—explanations for specific features of baby talk. Our goal is not to prove that a particular linguistic usage necessarily derives from a unique motivation, but rather to establish that baby talk is a coherent language style used both with children and adults, and that it arises for identifiable, logical reasons.

Pedagogy
A-C A-A

According to Aristotle's *Metaphysics*, "All men, by nature, desire to know." Whatever the truth about our inherent intellectual curiosity, adults do spend a good deal of energy explaining what they know to others. When we consider the features of baby talk, we find a good number of them are primarily pedagogical (though often coupled with other functions).

Consider phonology. The common baby talk techniques of speaking slowly, overenunciating, and overemphasizing one or two words in a sentence ("That's a *truck*, Katie. It's a *truck*") are tailor-made for the 1- or 2-year-old child trying to segment the speech stream into comprehensible units. Or when it comes to making lexical choices, many adults attempt (not overly successfully) to simplify labeling of the surrounding environment through onomatopoetic substitutions (e.g., *choo choo* for *train*) or use of familiar names for a more complex reality (e.g., calling a *chimpanzee* a *monkey*).

Syntactically, the use of nouns instead of pronouns ("Mommy wants Sarah to drink her milk") is a logical strategy for reinforcing people's names. The deictic declarative ("That's a ball") is an ideal way to teach labels. Other syntactic and conversational devices (such as, heightened grammaticality, shorter and simpler sentences, limitation of topic, and repetition) offer children clearer grammatical models than normally found in speech between adults. In much the same way, the practice of building upon what a child says (through expansion or recast) provides the developing speaker an immediate model linguistically related to what she has just said.

Turning to the pedagogical function of adult speech to adults, we find many of the same "special language" features surfacing. In the area of phonology, the fit is precise. Consider a minister preaching a Sunday sermon or a polished lecturer facing a large audience. The speech cadences are characterized by their slowness and clear enunciation (compare your conversation with a friend while waiting for a bus). At the same time, a highly successful rhetorical technique is to place particular emphasis on an important word or phrase.

Syntactically, the match is again close. A lecturing (or sermonizing) register is far more grammatical than everyday language. Among casual speakers addressing adult interlocutors who might not easily understand what is being said (e.g., non-native speakers of the language—or dialect), it is commonplace to use shorter and simpler sentences than when addressing compatriots fluent in the local patois.

In the realm of conversation, the specific features of baby talk are less manifest when adult language is used pedagogically. Although we occasionally repeat phrases for emphasis ("It was a sad day for America. A sad day indeed"), we do not pepper our pedagogical speech with a profusion of exact repetitions or expansions. Nonetheless, adult-to-adult language does have some "special forms" that serve a pedagogical function. An example is what we might call the "end run recast." A good conversationalist (or teacher) knows how to take what another person has said and turn it to pedagogical advantage. For example, if a student asks a question that is not really on the subject, an instructor might say, "That's an interesting question. It leads us to ask . . .," i.e., whatever the professor really wanted to talk about.

Control
A-C A-A

The control function encompasses a range of goals: from getting a person's attention, to establishing a social pecking order, to monopolizing a conversation. Only the first of these purposes is relevant in baby talk. The linguistic area in which it mainly crops up is phonology. Listen to mothers addressing infants. Typically you hear a greater range of frequencies than in adult-to-adult conversation. This range is motivated, at least in part, by a desire to get—and hold—the baby's attention. Intuitively, mothers seem to understand that babies attend more to novel (and varied) signals than to monotones. Another critical device—though hardly unique to baby talk—is to increase volume. A loud "Stop!" will generally get a toddler to halt in his tracks, even if he does not yet understand the meaning of the word.

In conversing with other adults, mature speakers exercise control through a number of linguistic means. To grab someone's attention, phonological variation in pitch, volume, or speed can be very effective. However, adult-to-adult conversations invite other sorts of "control" as well. One obvious example is the use of high-pitched speech (a very common feature of baby talk) in addressing hospital or nursing home patients whom caretakers perceive as similar to children in that they lack significant control over what is happening to them (Caporael & Culbertson, 1986). Another example is the conversational control that comes when speakers ask rhetorical questions and then proceed to answer them. Structurally, this technique is reminiscent of the tendency of parents with infants to carry the entire conversational burden, first asking questions and then providing answers. However, the functional motivation for this conversational monopoly is very different when used to address adults (where it is a form of control) than when used to address children (where it is a technique for modeling social exchange).

Affection
A-C A-A

As in the case of pedagogy, when adults select special language to express affection, they use many of the same forms to address adults as to address children. Much as parents are known for using high pitch and special pronunciations of certain words to indicate warm feelings for children (e.g., drawing out the vowel sound in the name of a favorite toy, as in, "Do you want to do a *pu-u-zzle* now?"), spouses and loved ones often employ similar language styles with each other. Comparable motivations lie behind the use of diminutives such as *kitty* (for *cat*) or *milkie* for *milk* with children and adults alike.

These same linguistic markers of affection appear in adult speech to non-linguistic creatures, including dogs, fish, or even plants. Hirsh-Pasek and Treiman (1982) invented the term *doggerel* to characterize the language style many adults use in addressing their canine companions. While at first blush, doggerel resembles baby talk, it turns out that only some of the linguistic features of baby talk appear in doggerel (e.g., use of high pitch, repetitions, supplying both questions and answers). Not surprisingly, these tend to be the baby talk features of affection and control. In talking with your dog, you would hardly be expected to use pedagogically-motivated linguistic forms (e.g., deictic declaratives).

Not all of the special language forms used to express affection are the same in adult-to-child speech as in adult-to-adult speech. An exclusive feature from child-directed speech is the echoing (as an expression of closeness) of nonce-forms children invent. For example, when at age 1;2 a child I know began calling milk *ki* (building upon the heavily aspirated *k* of *milk*), his family soon found themselves saying to the child, "Would you like some ki?" (Derivatively, husband and wife affectionately began using the word in conversations between themselves.)

Unique to adult-adult conversations expressing affection is the use of substitutions. Recall that adults speaking to children typically substitute one word (e.g., *choo choo*) for another presumed to be more difficult (e.g., *train*) or substitute proper nouns for pronouns ("Mommy wants Sarah to drink her milk") in an attempt to teach proper names. In adult language to adults, however, these same lexical substitutions serve not as forms of pedagogy, but as expressions of affection. If a man says to his wife, "Shall we ride the choo choo to Philadelphia?", he is not concerned that his mate might have difficulty pronouncing the initial *tr-* cluster in *train*. Similarly, if a woman says to her poodle, "Shall Mommy give Calvin some supper?", she is expressing affection, not trying to teach friend Calvin his name or hers. As you might guess, the affectionate tone of these locutions in adult-to-adult language itself derives from the common use of such substitutions in talking with babies, who are paradigmatic objects of affection.

Social Exchange
A-C A-C

The main function of a good deal of human conversation—both with adults and with children—is to keep social interaction going, even if we have nothing much to say. Typically, we accomplish this feat by ostensibly using language for some other purpose.

Not surprisingly, then, when we look at the use of "special language" for social exchange—especially in adult-to-child conversation, we find the same baby talk features we have already seen used for other language functions, especially pedagogy and the expression of affection. Among the features adults use phatically in their conversations with children are the imitation of words from the child's own repertoire (e.g., *fish* for *whale* or *ki* for *milk*). In the realm of syntax, adult speech is simpler, shorter, and even occasionally ungrammatical (e.g., "Would you like some up?"), with the goal of facilitating a response from the child. The same motivation underlies the appearance in conversation of frequent questions (but less frequent declaratives), repetitions both of one's own utterances and of what the child has just said, and heavy use of expansions and recasts.

Besides these familiar baby talk strategies, adults employ additional, less obvious conversational techniques for maintaining social interaction. One of these is to slip into the royal *we* ("Would we like to finish our spinach?"). Another is to restrict the choice of topics. Few 4-year-olds become involved when the conversation turns to budget deficits or the war on drugs. (One little 3-year-old temporarily developed the annoying habit of yelling "Stop it!" any time the conversation strayed beyond her comprehension.) A third tool parents use for "keeping the conversation going" with very young children is to assume the role of both speaker and hearer, first asking a question, next presuming the response, and then continuing the discourse from there ("Would you like me to burp you? Yes? I thought that was the problem. There, that's better").

In adult speech to other adults, the possibilities for maintaining conversation are vast. The most common lexical means is to pepper one's speech with *um*, *uh*, or *well*, hardly forms you would expect to find in speech to young children. At the conversational level, we accomplish this feat through paraphrase, recasting what we have already said until we figure out what we really want to talk about. While conversations with young children permit us to mark time through exact repetition, exchanges between adults must convey at least the semblance of novelty.

Information
A-C A-A

If you ask the average person what the purpose of language is, he or she will probably say, "To communicate information." While the sharing of information is indeed an important function of language, it is also the most neutral structurally. That is, strict conveyance of information does not require any "special language" forms. Not surprisingly, throughout the baby talk literature, no baby talk features are described exclusively as "communicating information." This is not to say that conversational exchanges that are strictly informational in character do not take place between parent and child (e.g., "Mom, I want cake"). The point is that the language itself has no particular distinguishing features of the sort we have been looking at. The same can be said for "information only" speech directed to adults.

WHERE DOES BABY TALK COME FROM?

How do the particular features of baby talk arise? Are they rooted in our biology (like a baby's sucking reflex)? Are they "natural" responses to situations? Or are they learned behaviors? To help answer this question, we turn from language to a very different realm of human behavior: art.

In talking about the history of art, André Malraux has argued (1949-1950) that the work of artists is less a response to the external world (or our perceptions of it) than a response to other art. We paint the head of Christ a particular way less because that is what we think he looked like than because of the ways in which other artists have painted him.

In much the same vein, the structural manifestations of baby talk derive less from our biological responses to children than from the baby talk we hear modeled by others. You do not need to be a parent to know how adults are "supposed" to converse with young children (e.g., Snow, 1972). We learn from our own parents, from the family next door, from television sit-coms. In turn, our children learn from us the components of a baby talk register, sometimes when as young as age 2 or 3 (Dunn & Kendrick, 1982). As with any knowledge, we may choose to retain or reject behavior patterns we see in others ("If I have a child, I will never say *choo choo* or *doggie*"). The choices themselves derive more from the adult language we hear around us than from our spontaneous expressions of feeling about infants and toddlers.

DOES BABY TALK HELP?

Should parents use baby talk in addressing children? Does it do any harm? While very occasionally, use of an isolated baby talk feature may put a temporary damper on the emergence of a specific linguistic construction (see Chapter 6), baby talk as a speech register has never been shown to hamper linguistic growth.

But what about positive benefits?

When linguists have asked whether baby talk is a beneficial speech style, they have been concerned exclusively with whether the use of baby talk features by parents correlates with a child's subsequent development of conversation, phonology, meaning, or especially syntax. In the coming chapters, we will explore the issue of the pedagogical effects of baby talk.

By now we recognize, however, that pedagogy is but one function of baby talk. Baby talk also is an instrument of control and a means of expressing affection. While the pedagogical effects of baby talk are best measured through the child's subsequent language development, the effects of these other two functions must be assessed through the adult speaker: *Does* she gain control? *Does* her language express her emotions?

If the effects of baby talk on a child's developing language are difficult to prove, the effects of baby talk on adults and their emotional interaction with children are even harder to measure.

Successful control and interaction are highly relative accomplishments. The *laissez faire* father may be satisfied if his son looks up when he calls, while a more strict disciplinarian may insist upon his son's undivided attention before judging the exchange a success. Every parent must individually evaluate the efficacy of baby talk, especially when it functions for control or as an expression of affection. Human language allows us to fill the same functions through many forms. One parent may find special language features (such as the use of diminutives) to be a comfortable way of expressing affection, while another parent might supplement normal language with lots of hugs and kisses.

What about the fourth language function of baby talk: to promote social interaction? Does this use of baby talk foster language development in the child? Does it benefit the parent? The answer to both questions is "yes." Human language grows out of people's need to interact with one another. The child needs to learn the formal words and constructions that make this interchange possible. The adult needs to feel that the infant in his arms is a real human with whom he can communicate, even though the child knows only how to gurgle and cry.

To see how language arises—for both parent and child—out of the need for social conversation, we turn to Chapter 4.

4

The Language Duet:
Conversation and Imitation

On days when I arrive at work early, I often see Mercedes in my office, vacuuming the rug and emptying the trash cans. Mercedes is a delightful woman. She is a college graduate and the mother of two teenage daughters. When we meet, I say "Good morning. How are you?" With a big smile she responds, "Good morning. Fine."

End of conversation.

We both want to say more but do not know how. Mercedes is from Nicaragua and speaks almost no English. My Spanish is nonexistent. After our morning ritual, we turn silent and part. We literally do not know what else to say to each other.

THE CONVERSATIONAL IMPERATIVE

When in the presence of other people, we have a natural tendency to talk. Shyness and socialization aside ("Don't talk to strangers" "Don't speak until you are spoken to"), we find it awkward to be with another sentient being for any period of time and remain mum. We might call this drive to speak the *conversational imperative*.

Think about the last time you were at an airport waiting for a plane that was delayed. For the first 10 or 20 minutes, perhaps you kept your thoughts to yourself. But, as time dragged on, and the cluster of people at the gate shared in your mounting frustration, you may well have remarked on your concern to the woman in the next seat. By the time the plane actually arrived, you had learned all about her grandchildren, and she was privy to your fear of flying.

Comparable scenarios occur at bus stops, on trains, in stalled elevators—anytime strangers are thrown together in relatively close quarters. But, the conversational imperative also spurs communication between people who already know each other. Long silences (at least in contemporary American culture) are generally seen as isolating. We use conversation as a bridge for human companionship, even when we have nothing much to say. Such linguistic fillers are as common around the family dinner table as they are at cocktail parties.

This conversational imperative also accounts in large part for the "conversations" we have with pets. We saw in the last chapter that our language with canine companions is a means of expressing affection. However, our patter while walking the dog in the morning or watching her eat in the evening derives as much from our urge to talk to someone—even someone who cannot answer back.

It is this basic desire to interact with another sentient being that drives our earliest "conversations" with children. Happily, our desire to talk provides the developing child an ideal medium for learning language.

THE CONVERSATIONAL ROOTS OF LANGUAGE

A question that has gnawed at me for years is *why* children learn language. Obviously, children are extremely curious and tend to absorb new information like sponges. But acquiring human language is no small task. Even given our biological predisposition to become language users, neophytes still must devote considerable energies to learning how to contort their mouths into *w*'s and *l*'s, to distinguishing between *by* and *buy* ("Shall we go by the store and buy some apples?"), and to figuring out when to stick *do* in front of a sentence (as in, "Do you want some cheese?"). We know that many children actually practice the new pronunciations, words, and constructions they are learning (e.g., Nelson, 1989).

The "why" of language learning is obviously a multidimensional issue. Children learn because they are curious, because they are imitative, because they are bored. But, children also learn—and especially learn language—because they want to connect up with other people, and those other people are using language as a bridge to social interaction.

Human language is deeply rooted in the social duet between infant and caregiver (see Snow, 1977, 1986). The language stream coming from a mother (or father or grandparent) to a 6-week-old baby is hardly pedagogically motivated. Rather, it is the natural accompaniment to nurturing activities and developing friendship. Over the months, this duet evolves in function and in the child's level of participation.

Early Conversations

How does the conversational duet begin? Intuitively, we might assume that the earliest language "exchanges" are one-sided: The adult initiates, the child stares back in silence, and then the adult continues as if the child had responded ("Is that a block you have in your hand? Yes, you're right, it is"). Gradually (so the logic goes), parents find meaning in their babies' increasing vocalizations, and before you know it, the children have begun joining in on the language game.

Reality turns out to involve much more joint participation. From the earliest months of life, babies not only respond with gurgles and coos to adult patter, but also initiate conversational exchanges to which adults then respond. Sometimes it is the parent who opens the duet, sometimes the child. Is it important who starts? Probably not. What *does* matter is that someone gets the ball rolling. Thanks to the conversational imperative, even if your baby is the silent type, you will, quite naturally, start talking (much as you would to your cocker spaniel). The advantage is that, unlike the dog, the child will eventually respond.

One of the first lessons that children learn from the early conversational duet is that language is a dialogue: First it is my turn, then it is yours. Turn-taking routines actually serve a dual function in very young children's linguistic development. Besides teaching children that language is a verbal game of volleyball, the exchange offers babies valuable experience in vocalizing. In a study of the effects of turn-taking on 3-month-old infants, Bloom, Russell, and Wassenberg (1987) found that the more turn-taking babies engaged in, the more language-like their vocalizations were. Note that we said "language-like." The average 3-month-old is not yet making identifiable babbling sounds. However, just as babbling influences the first phases of real phonological and lexical development (see Vihman, Macken, Miller, Simmons, & Miller, 1985, for a review of the literature), early vocal practice may well help facilitate babbling.

Sometimes the conversation bogs down. You address your 1-year-old ("Would you like some cheese?") and get no response. What do you do next? The most common answer for parents is simply to say it again: "Would you like some cheese?" (pause) "Would you like some cheese?" Such repetitions play an important pedagogical function: The more times children hear sentences clearly modeled, the more language learning is facilitated. However, especially with children who have not yet begun using syntax, an equally important function of repetition is phatic communication giving adults something to say. As any parent of a young child discovers, finding topics of conversation with a partner whose active linguistic repertoire is limited to *no*, *daddy*, *truck*, and *milk* can prove challenging indeed. Quite naturally, we lapse into repetition.

Emerging Dialogue

Once a child can articulate a handful of words (typically between 12 and 16 months), the real dialogue begins. Parents no longer need to supply both query and answer, but can respond to their child's own interest.

Child: Duck.
Adult: My, what a lovely duck you have. Does he know how to talk?
Child: Quack.
Adult: Yes, Michael. The duck goes "quack, quack."

As children get older and more linguistically sophisticated parental responses zero in on children's emerging intent:

Child: Broom falled down.
Adult: Yes, the broom fell down, didn't it?
or
Child: Broom falled down.
Adult: Shall we pick the broom up and put it back where it belongs?

In the first exchange, the parent expands upon the child's utterance, rounding out the syntax and, *en passant*, correcting the grammar. In the second case, the parent *recasts* the subject matter into the next phase of conversation. However beneficial these expansions and recasts are to children's emerging language (see Chapter 7 for details), we should not forget that parents benefit as well. Such responses offer adults natural ways of continuing conversational (and therefore social) give-and-take with children. No longer is the parent stuck with repetition as the only way of filling the conversational void.

Who sets the tone of conversation? Sometimes the adult, sometimes the child. Smolak and Weinraub (1983), for example, analyzed the speech patterns of mothers to their 2-year-old daughters, half of whom were characterized as having a high level of language (more than 100 spoken words, consistent use of basic syntax) and half of whom had less developed language (fewer than 60 words, no real syntax). Regardless of their children's language abilities, both groups of mothers had the same general conversational characteristics. The authors do note, however, that mothers of the more linguistically advanced children did tend to talk more—and as Wells (1980) has shown, the amount a mother speaks is a good predictor of a child's rate of language acquisition.

The potential role of children in driving conversation is illustrated in a study by Yoder and Kaiser (1989). Comparing mother-child conversations when the children were first an average of 22 months old (T_1) with comparable data collected five months later (T_2), the authors argue that the mothers' style of language at time T_2 typically reflects the child's style at time T_1. For example, children who at T_1 use multi-word utterances may be encouraging their mothers subsequently to ask more questions that, in turn, elicits more language.

As children grow, so do their conversational needs. A number of researchers (e.g., Cross, 1977) have argued that mothers "fine tune" their speech to match the changing conversational abilities of their offspring. However, other studies (e.g., Retherford, Schwartz, & Chapman, 1981) point out that it is often the child who "tunes in" to the mother by growing linguistically to match the content and frequency of structures she models in her own language.

CONVERSATION IN CONTEXT
Cultural Customs

Who spends time in conversation with young children? In the United States, the answer is overwhelmingly "women." However, middle-class fathers are becoming increasingly involved in child care activities, and "house husband" is losing its status as an oxymoron. The more time fathers spend interacting with their children, the greater influence they are likely to have on their children's language development. Already, men in dual-income families are beginning to take up the conversational role. Work by Ackerman-Ross (1985) has shown that fathers whose children are in nursery school all day average an additional hour each weekday and two additional hours each weekend day talking with their child than fathers whose children (and wives) are home during the week.

In Chapters 5, 6, and 7, we will review available data on phonological, lexical, and grammatical aspects of fathers' speech to young children. For now, suffice it to say that while early studies suggested marked differences between male and female speech to children (notably, a relative paucity of baby talk features in language from fathers), more recent research has been yielding conflicting results. Some of the discrepancies probably reflect failure to control for the same variables across experiments (especially the age of the child being addressed). However, the explanation may also lie in the changing social times.

Another dimension to the gender question is how we speak to male versus female children. In some subcultures, parents maintain that differential linguistic treatment is appropriate: Little girls should be spoken to sweetly and gently, little boys should be addressed more directly (i.e., less baby talk). In contemporary America, most middle-class families assume their conversation with children is gender-neutral. The reality of the situation may surprise you. A number of studies suggest that the average middle-class parent does *not* talk the same way to little girls as to little boys.

What do we mean by "the same"? Start with a simple measure: amount of talk. Results from a variety of researchers indicate that mothers interact verbally more with their young daughters than with their sons. Moss (1967) found that mothers were more likely to imitate the vocalizations of infant daughters than of infant sons.

Goldberg and Lewis (1969) note that mothers vocalized to their 1-year-old daughters more than to their 1-year-old sons. Cherry and Lewis (1976) report that mothers talked more to their 2-year-old daughters than to their 2-year-old sons. Such differences may well be significant for subsequent language acquisition because other studies have shown that the amount parents imitate children's early vocalizations (Hardy-Brown & Plomin, 1985) or the amount of speech addressed to a child (Wells, 1980) is predictive of the child's rate of early language acquisition.

Before exhorting parents to talk more to their sons, we need to remember that language is a two-way street. Because child vocalizations tend to elicit adult responses, it may well be that the real reason mothers vocalize less to their little boys than to their little girls is that the little boys, at least as young infants, do not themselves vocalize as much (Lewis, 1969; Lewis & Freedle, 1973). (A curious side-note: While Cameron, Livson, & Bayley [1967] have reported a close correlation between amount of vocalization in infant girls and subsequent intelligence, no such correlation was found for boys.)

Which parent does most of the talking? Researchers have generally found that mothers tend to talk more to their young children than do fathers. Golinkoff and Ames (1979) report that when fathers, mothers, and their 19-month-old sons or daughters were together in a free-play situation, fathers did less of the conversational turn-taking than did mothers. Hladik and Edwards (1984), studying parental conversation with 2-year-olds and 3 1/2-year olds, found that mothers talked more with children (of either sex) than did fathers and more often initiated conversations. (Fathers tended to react to what their children had said.) In the same vein, Rondal (1980) reports that mothers of French children between the ages of 1;6 and 3;0 did more of the talking than did fathers.

Despite common lore that women do not let their interlocutors get a word in edgewise, according to Greif (1980), fathers, not mothers, interrupt their children's speech more often. What is more, Greif found that both fathers and mothers were more likely to interrupt the speech of their daughters than of their sons. Why? One possible reason is that because boys tend to be slightly slower in language development than girls, parents may hesitate to interrupt speech that is more difficult to produce. Parents of children going through

41

periods of stuttering (and these children are more likely to be boys) know the importance of exercising patience while the words are coming out.

What about differences between the ways in which mothers and fathers address their sons and daughters, respectively? In their study of children attending day care programs, Ackerman-Ross and Khanna (1989) report that while mothers spent equal language time with their sons and daughters, they tended to play a bit more with their daughters. Meanwhile, fathers spent more language time and more play time with their sons.

Besides looking at volume of talk and at turn-taking styles, we can ask what parents talk about with their children. Weintraub (1977), comparing the speech of mothers and fathers to children between 3;0 and 4;4, found that mothers were twice as likely as fathers to use stock phrases (e.g., "Oh, my goodness" or "Thank you"). Weintraub suggests that mothers use such phrases to keep the conversational flow going with their less-than-fluent interlocutors. A study by Weitzman, Birns, and Friend (1985) of conversations with children between the ages of 2;6 and 3;6 found marked differences in the language mothers addressed to males and females. Sons were consistently more verbally stimulated than daughters (on such measures as the number of questions mothers asked, and the attention mothers paid to explicit descriptions of emotional states, to clothing of characters in a story, and to time and number specification).

Work by O'Brien and Nagle (1987) on parents' conversations with toddlers suggests that the toys a child plays with rather than the sex of the child determines the amount and character of language that parents of either sex address to either sex child. The language that parents addressed to their sons and daughters alike was far richer when the play-object was a doll than when the toy in question was a truck or a car. The authors conclude that

> [t]he context of doll play appears to provide a situation that promotes the active teaching of language to toddlers [e.g., more and longer utterances, frequent labelling of objects, a high proportion of questions (particularly yes-no questions), a great variety of words, a high ratio of nouns to pronouns].
> ... [G]irls' more frequent selection of dolls as toys [compared with boys' more frequent selection of trucks and cars] may

open increased opportunities for them to learn and practice language and may therefore contribute to girls' early language proficiency. (p. 277)

On the face of things the data on parental conversation with male and female children seem contradictory: While some studies suggest that girls receive more verbal stimulation, others imply boys are the main linguistic benefactors. As we will see in the coming chapters, the data on speech to sons versus daughters (and from mothers versus fathers) are still in need of refinement. It may turn out, for example, that age is an important variable, and that American parents are more likely to lavish linguistic attention on infant and toddler girls, and then to shift (or at least equalize) their focus on preschool aged boys. In their review of the literature on sex differences in language development, Maccoby and Jacklin (1974) report that among middle-class Americans, girls appear to have a verbal advantage over boys before age 3 and after age 11, but not in between. It will be interesting to explore what role parents might play in this linguistic equalization of the sexes between ages 3 and 11.

Family Circumstances

Conversational patterns with children are also intimately linked to particular family circumstances. Educational level of the parents, especially the mother, predicts rate of early language development (e.g., Wells, 1984). This finding is hardly surprising. The conversation of educated parents tends to be rich and linguistically demanding, modeling a high standard for becoming part of the family linguistic community.

Besides education, the most important family variable affecting parental conversation is numbers: Is this an only child? Is the child a twin (or triplet)? If there are older siblings, how much older are they?

The impact of numbers is obvious. The more children parents have to care for at the same time, the less linguistic attention they can offer individual children. With several young children in the family, not only does the *amount* of conversation with each child go down, but the very *character* of the language addressed to children changes. Not surprisingly, the conversation children begin using reflects, in return, the style of talk addressed to them.

Consider the realities of having twins. Suppose, for the sake of argument, that an average mother spends a total of 120 minutes a day in conversation with her 4-month-old. With twins, the number of available minutes per child immediately drops to 60. Indeed, many studies of adult speech to twins (e.g., Lytton, Conway, & Sauvé, 1977; Conway, Lytton, & Pysh, 1980; Tomasello, Mannle, & Kruger, 1986) confirm that parents of twins address less language to each twin than parents of only children address to singletons of the same age.

The conversational content is likely to differ as well. Tomasello et al.'s study found that mothers of 21-month-old twins spent less than half the amount of time in joint attention vignettes with their children (e.g., playing with an airplane, talking about a toy bear) than did mothers of only children. Moreover, mothers of twins made the following linguistic variations.

* "led" the conversation twice as frequently as mothers of only children
* used sentences that were shorter in length, contained more imperatives, and had fewer comments and questions
* restricted their naming of objects to directive utterances (e.g., "Give me the ball"), almost never talking about an object in a non-directive way (e.g., "What a pretty blue ball")
* continued to use short sentences to their children, even as they grew older

Comparing the conversational style of the twins with conversations of only children of the same age, the authors report that in a 15-minute session, the twins used language in the following ways.

* produced only 1/4 the number of words as did only children (an average of 34 vs. 130)
* used much smaller vocabularies (an average of 8 vs. 47 different words)
* engaged in less than half the number of conversations (an average of 5.2 vs. 13.6)

Other studies have shown that while the amount of speech twins use may be less than that of singletons, twins typically speak at a faster clip. Competing for adult attention, twins often omit consonants or entire syllables (see Savic, 1980; Hay, Prior, Collett, & Williams, 1987).

The problem that parents—and twins—encounter in finding ample conversational "air time" is but one extreme of the more common situation occurring in families that include several young children. With only so many hours in the day, how can parents appropriately tailor their language to both, say, a 1-year-old and a 4-year-old (and still get supper on the table, the dishes done, and the house even vaguely cleaned)?

Oftentimes, the younger child ends up conversationally short-changed. A number of researchers have reported (e.g., Lewis & Feiring, 1982; Woollet, 1986) that when older siblings are present, fewer verbal exchanges take place between parents and the younger child. Nelson (1981) points out that when two siblings are together with their mother, the mother's speech tends to be directive and centered around the activity at hand. When mothers are alone with one child, the maternal language is likely to be more pedagogical. Work by Jones and Adamson (1987) confirms these findings. Another study (Wellen, 1985), this time of mothers with 2-year-olds and 4-year-olds, found that when both children were present for the reading of a story, the older child responded to more than half of the mother's questions before the younger child even had a chance to speak. The younger child's overall linguistic participation in such three-party conversations was less than half of what it was when reading stories with the mother alone.

How do such conversational patterns affect young children's emerging language? For many years now, researchers have agreed that first-born children tend to develop the rudiments of language faster than subsequent siblings (e.g., McCarthy, 1954). But, there is more to the story.

All other factors being equal, first-born children typically begin acquiring language via a different strategy than subsequent closely aged siblings. While first-borns are likely to adopt a *referential* approach to early vocabulary acquisition (learning many individual names for things), later born children lean toward a more *expressive* approach, filling their early lexicon with social words and phrases such as *no, please, I want that,* or *good-bye* (Nelson, 1973; Jones & Adamson, 1987). Twins also tend to be *expressive* in their language

45

acquisition patterns (Savic, 1980). Analysis of the language adults address to young children suggests that children's strategies reflect the type of language they hear: "referential mothers" are likely to beget referential children, and "expressive mothers" beget expressive children.

A common explanation of this divergence in parental conversational modes is that first-time parents favor referential language because of understandable uncertainty about their children's development. By frequently naming objects, parents foster object-naming behavior in their children that, in turn, reassures parents that language acquisition is progressing normally. By the time a second child appears on the scene, these same parents typically relax and include more social give-and-take in their conversation.

Whatever truth dwells in these arguments, we should not ignore the very real issue of differential demands on the time of parents with one child versus parents with two or more. By Parkinson's Law, work expands to fill the time available of *both* types of parents. Yet, in the end, parents of only children have more opportunity to direct age-appropriate language to young children (including names for things) than do parents with more than one youngster to contend with.

Child-Centered Variables

However much biology and environment influence language development, the person learning to talk is a unique child. Some children are shy, others aggressive. One child will be cautious while another may be a daredevil. What does a child's personality have to do with adult and child conversational patterns? As we have already seen, speakers of all ages naturally tend to adjust their language to what they perceive to be the abilities of their interlocutor. If a child is not talking much—for whatever reason—it is easy for adults to slip into more restricted conversation in return. With such children, it is important to remember that much of child development takes place beneath the surface. A once-quiet child may suddenly blossom linguistically if the nurturing conditions have been strong.

Do parents adjust their conversational style to suit the temperament of their children? In many cases, yes. In a longitudinal study of the language addressed to 10-, 14-, and 18-month-old infants, Smolak (1987) found that several aspects of child temperament (e.g., whining, not concentrating on a play activity) correlated with certain continuing verbal strategies from mothers (e.g., a high level of self-repetitions and of directives).

Often the attitude a child assumes toward physical activity is mirrored in his approach to language learning. Consider the changes my son Aneil underwent during the transition from toddler to preschooler. Between the ages of 1;0 and 2;6, the boy was extremely cautious about his person and his movements. He was careful not to spill food on himself, and I never needed to remind him to go down the steps carefully—he automatically did so. At the same time, he was not a risk-taker in his language. If he was not able to pronounce a word correctly, he simply would not attempt it—unlike other children who freely omit sounds or syllables (e.g., saying *nana* for *banana*) or substitute easier sounds for more difficult ones (e.g., *dat* for *that*). Not Aneil. He would point, grunt—anything but get it wrong. When he turned 2;6, suddenly his personality changed. The little boy now insisted on going down the high slide by himself, descending the stairs backwards with his eyes closed—and taking linguistic risks. He overgeneralized irregular inflections (saying *falled* for *fell* and *mans* for *men*) and came up with novel syntax (e.g., "Aneil do not going home") that he clearly had never heard.

THE QUESTION OF IMITATION

How do children progress from single-word users to syntactic dynamos? One vital technique (admittedly, exploited more by some personality types than others) is to imitate the conversation adults address to them. Imitation has long been a taboo notion among child language specialists. Yet, when we look at imitation in context of conversational exchange, we begin to understand its function in language acquisition.

Nature vs. Nurture Revisited

In talking about the difference between development, acquisition, and learning, we contrasted the end points of the nature-nurture spectrum. While Chomsky has argued that human language is paradigmatically a creative production, Skinner emphasizes the role of modeling in individual language acquisition and use.

47

For more than 20 years, studies of language acquisition in America have largely presupposed the Chomskyan position on creativity. That is, students of acquisition have argued that morphology and syntax emerge not from memorization but from growing control over a developing linguistic system. Time and again, references in the literature to overgeneralized plurals like *mans* and *childrens,* or overgeneralized past tenses like *falled* or *wented* are cited as evidence that children do not learn language by imitation.

Without a doubt, children are not automata, mindlessly mimicking the language they hear. Yet, it is equally true that the conversation addressed to children—and their imitation thereof—are vital components in linguistic development. Let us see how these two seemingly opposed perspectives of imitation and creativity can be reconciled.

Ma Please Peel One More Time Guys

In the mid-1970s, Lois Bloom and her colleagues (Bloom, Hood, & Lightbrown, 1974) published an article entitled "Imitation in Language Development: If, When, and Why." The paper approached the issue of imitation quite cautiously. Studying the speech patterns of children just making the transition from single words to syntax, the authors concluded that imitation was sometimes an important device for reinforcing structures the children were about to learn. For example, a child on the verge of learning the word *foot* might first use it imitatively before speaking it spontaneously. Similarly, a child in the process of learning action-location relationships (e.g., *sit down, fall over*) might tend to imitate such models in adult speech.

While the data speak for themselves, they belie the far broader role that imitation plays in the language acquisition of many children (see Clark, 1977; Snow, 1978; Leonard, Chapman, Rowan, & Weiss, 1983; and especially Speidel & Nelson, 1989). Children listen to adults all day long. If you observe the conversation adults direct to children, you cannot help but notice how repetitive it is. We repeat ourselves both for the sake of pedagogy and, as we said earlier in this chapter, because it is genuinely hard to keep thinking of new things to say to a 2- or 3-year-old. Not surprisingly, children begin repeating what they hear, often combining imitation with originality.

Here are three examples from one little boy at age 2;9. An avid

Sesame Street watcher, the child would sometimes view a single videotape of the program more than a dozen times. One day he was playing in the sandbox, and his shoes became filled with sand. As his mother began to empty them, he mischievously muttered what sounded for all the world like "puce shoes." Puce shoes? He said it again. And again. It turned out that the child had learned the color puce from a vignette on *Sesame Street*, in which Maria tries on every pair of shoes in the shop, and finally emerges with a prized pair of puce shoes. Neither parent had ever spoken the word in the boy's presence.

Or consider this conversation the child had with his mother on the way home from nursery school. Passing a squirrel scampering up a tree, the preschooler paused and said, "Have a nose, have a tail, have a feets." The origin of *feets* as a creative overgeneralized plural is obvious. But the use of *have* (instead of the correct singular *has*) and the inappropriate use of the article (*a*) with *feets* are not cases of creativity. Rather, they were examples of imitation. One of the conversational games the mother often played with the boy was a question-answer routine in which she would say, "Does a squirrel have a tail?", "Does a car have a bumper?", and so on. Through imitation of the routine, the child had ended up with an incorrect verb agreement and mistaken patterning of article with noun. What he had mastered, though, were the rudiments of conversational frames.

The third example of combined imitation and creativity is my favorite. Driving home in the car one afternoon, the little boy was hungry, so his mother handed him a half-peeled banana. As they drove, he ate down to the peel and wanted help in extricating the rest of the fruit: "Ma peel please one more time guys." The pieces all came from adult sources: "Please" had been painstakingly taught. "One more time" was a gummed-together, memorized phrase he had heard from adults over and again ("Would you say that one more time when your mouth is empty?"). "Guys" was a form of address he had picked up at school that week. Yet, the combination was wholly unique.

Imitation as Conversation

The fact that most children, at one point or another in their first few years, are prolific imitators in no way detracts from the creative component of language learning. Pedagogically, imitation is an obvious way to get an initial fix on vocabulary and grammar. (Those of us who learned foreign languages in school through the conversational approach can attest to the usefulness of this method.) But imitation in children is not simply a way to learn language components. It also provides a technique for making conversation.

In Chapter 3, we talked about *repetitions, expansions,* and *recasts* as examples of the special talk that adults use in conversing with young children. Repetitions of child speech by adults are imitations by another name. Expansions and recasts are versions of imitations of a child's previous utterance. All three can function to keep up social interchange.

Given the significant amount of imitation (exact or embellished) that adults do of their children's utterances, it is hardly surprising to find children imitating their parents' speech as well. If parental imitation of child speech serves a phatic function, child imitation of parental speech can be used toward the same end. Pedagogy is often an indirect effect of, rather than the primary motivation for, such imitation by children. Language imitation here serves the same role as children "driving" the car or "helping" to cook dinner. Through imitative behavior, children learn to participate in their parents' social universe.

In a sense, all of the language that adults address to young children falls under the rubric "conversation." However, it is useful to focus on the individual structural components of language—sound, meaning, and syntax—to understand *how* the conversation of parents impacts upon children's growing language. Therefore, we turn in Chapters 5, 6, and 7 to the influence parents have in these three specific linguistic domains.

5

I'd Know That Voice Anywhere: Modeling Sounds

A number of years back, I sat in a lecture hall, listening to a renowned French linguist speak on a problem of dialectology. The lecture was in English, and I was duly impressed by the speaker's fluency. Had I not known him to be a Frenchman, I would have sworn he was a native speaker of British U (for "upperclass") English.

Suddenly, in the midst of an elegant sentence, the professor uttered the word *first*, and appeared for all the world like a Brooklyn cab driver. For the word came out sounding like *foist* (rhyming with *hoist*).

Why such an aberration? Some hurried research revealed that near the end of World War II, this distinguished scholar had joined the flood of refugees entering the United States. He remained in New York for nearly a decade before returning to Paris. Despite his legendary linguistic talents, he obviously acquired a souvenir of his years in the Big Apple.

Anyone who has traveled through the United States or to other parts of the English-speaking world knows how easily and unconsciously speakers absorb components of the local dialect. After a week in Ireland, many an America tourist adds a lilt to her speech. Six months in England is sure to monkey with your vowels. My favorite example is a friend who was a native of Virginia. Raised in Norfolk, he spent four years as an undergraduate at Columbia University (in New York City) and then three years at Harvard Business School in Cambridge, Massachusetts. By the time he received his MBA, his accent reminded me of Neopolitan ice cream: some straight chocolate, some vanilla or strawberry, and some truly unique blends.

The most noticeable—and lasting—effect parents have on children's language is on their sound structure: the way children pronounce vowels, the cadence of their questions, the rate of the speech stream itself. Most of us remember our embarrassment (even fury) as teenagers when we answered the telephone and the caller mistook us for our mother or father: "You sound just like your dad," they would say, and we seethed with indignation at our loss of individuality.

The evolution of a child's phonology makes the case *par excellence* for the role of imitation in language learning. Of course, children's imitations are hardly limited to language. Consider how many other aspects of development closely shadow parental (and community) style. Children naturally tend to adopt the gait, posture, and even style of applause they see modeled by their parents.

Parental influence on kinesics often does not become evident for a number of years. Likewise, it takes time for the vocal apparatus to mature into its adult configuration and for the growing child's gross motor movements to settle into adult patterns. Like a stew that must cook for hours before the flavors meld, the most lasting effects of parents' phonology upon their children's evolving sound systems may take years to surface fully.

PHONOLOGICAL FEATURES OF BABY TALK

While the influence of parents' phonological patterns on children's speech is slow to reach full flower, an early role for adult speech patterns is nonetheless evident in other ways. In Chapter 3, we noted that high pitch and considerable pitch variation are typical in adult speech to infants. Expanding this list, Fernald and Simon (1984) have identified seven features distinguishing the speech of German mothers to their babies from mothers' speech to other adults: Besides higher pitch and wide pitch excursions, the authors include longer pauses, shorter utterances, more prosodic repetition, expanded intonation contours, and whispering.

Why this bundle of features? Fernald and Simon pinpoint essentially the same four language functions—pedagogy, control, affect, and social exchange—that we identified in Chapter 3. Pedagogically, the mother's prosodic patterns help the infant distinguish her speech signal from surrounding language or noise, add acoustical integrity to a single utterance through continuous pitch excursions, and aid in eventual speech comprehension through frequent repetition of the same acoustic pattern. These phonological devices offer a form of control in that they help maintain the baby's attention. The same baby talk features provide a medium for expressing affection and facilitating social exchange by assisting the infant to distinguish her mother's voice from other speech signals. An earlier study by Mehler, Bertoncini, Barrière, and Jassik-Gerschenfeld (1978) demonstrated that a 1-month-old can single out his mother's voice when she uses the rich phonological variation characterizing baby talk, but not when she speaks in a monotone.

Harder to prove is whether these prosodic features directed to infants eventually help or not—we obviously cannot ask the beneficiaries. But, we can find out if infants like to hear baby talk. Fernald (1985), in a study of 4-month-olds, found that subjects preferred listening to the varied phonological contours of baby talk (in contrast to the more even-keeled language typically spoken among adults). In fact, in another study, the author and her colleagues (Fernald & Kuhl, 1987) discovered that when they altered the speech signal, removing all syntactic and semantic information and only maintaining the characteristic pitch contours of baby talk, 4-month-olds preferred synthesized baby talk pitch contours to comparable contours of adults "speaking" to other adults.

PITCHING LANGUAGE TO INFANTS

Of all phonological aspects of baby talk, probably the most acoustically prominent—and definitely the one most commented upon—is the use of higher pitch (see Remick, 1976; Garnica, 1977). Ask the man-on-the-street to demonstrate how you are "supposed" to talk to babies, and you are almost guaranteed a high-pitched vocalization in response. This high pitch is hard to suppress. An exercise I commonly give students in my language acquisition classes is a naturalistic observation: Record a play session with a child between the ages of 2 and 4, transcribe the conversation, and analyze the results. Each year, after completing the assignment, students sheepishly admit that despite concerted efforts to speak normally, they slipped into a high pitched voice.

Some linguists (e.g., Grieser & Kuhl, 1988) maintain that the prosodic features of baby talk, including higher overall pitch, are universal. Functionally, higher pitch fills many roles: marking out the mother's speech, giving salience to major linguistic boundaries, getting the child's attention, conveying affection. And indeed, use of higher pitch to babies occurs in such diverse language communities as American English (Garnica, 1977), German (Fernald & Kuhl, 1987), Spanish (Blount & Padgug, 1977), and Mandarin Chinese (Grieser & Kuhl, 1988).

The case of Mandarin Chinese is especially interesting because of the phonological structure of Chinese itself. Unlike most European languages, Chinese is a "tonal" language, meaning that the same phoneme combination, pronounced with different pitch contours, has different meanings. For example, the Chinese word for "day"— ha[\]o—is distinguished from ha[\/]o meaning "good" only by the tonal structure of the vowels (i.e., falling tone versus falling-plus-rising) (Lyons, 1971). Because pitch variations make for differences in meaning, we might expect that Mandarin-speaking mothers would steer clear of pitch change as a device for demarcating conversation with infants. Yet, as a study by Grieser and Kuhl (1988) shows, the amount of pitch increase found in the baby talk of Mandarin-speaking mothers to their 2-month-old infants very closely approximated acoustical findings for English-speaking and German-speaking mothers. The authors conclude that

> [t]he acoustic features that are most salient
> [such as higher pitch] are likely to be the ones
> that are "universal" in maternal speech to in-
> fants across diverse languages and may well
> serve a common purpose. (p. 17)

It all makes sense. But, before closing the books on the question, we need to ask (like the minister before finalizing a marriage) if anyone objects.

SOUND IN CONTEXT
Cultural Customs

By now we know to expect that cultural circumstances can alter the "normal" style of language addressed to children. Our case in point involving phonology concerns the average pitch levels used by speakers of Quiche Mayan (a language spoken in western Guatemala) when addressing young children. Studying the speech of Quiche mothers to children between the ages of 1;10 and 2;6, Ratner and Pye (1984) found that compared with speech between adults, mother-to-child speech had either the same or even *lower* pitch.

Why?

The explanation lies in the mapping of cultural presuppositions onto language features in the Quiche community. In Mayan languages, adult speakers are reported to vary their pitch level depending upon the status of the person they are addressing, "high pitch being used to listeners of high status, and low pitch to listeners of lower status, at least with female speakers" (p. 520). Ratner and Pye hypothesize that infants are at the bottom of the status ladder, and therefore, are addressed in relatively low-pitched speech.

The data from Quiche constitute evidence for our observation in Chapter 3 that baby talk is at least as much a response to baby talk as it is to babies. Whatever natural tendencies we might have to raise our pitch when speaking to infants, our baby talk most directly reflects the baby talk we hear used by other adults in the culture.

Family Circumstances

Turning from cultural variables to family-related issues, let us begin with the question of education. Many highly educated parents do not believe they manifest phonological baby talk features in their speech. (In fact, highly educated parents sometimes claim not to use *any* baby talk features.) Even cursory observation of university professors talking to their infants disproves such proclamations. Yet, it may well be the case that the particular *features* of baby talk a parent uses vary with educational background. For example, while a highly educated mother may regularly place heavy emphasis on one or two words in a sentence (e.g., "Would you like some *juice?*"), perhaps her use of heightened pitch levels will be less exaggerated than those of mothers with less formal education.

How does the sex—of child or parent—affect parental vocalization to children? We noted in Chapter 4 that American mothers tend to vocalize more to daughters than to sons (e.g., Moss, 1967; Goldberg & Lewis, 1969). Yet, *amount* of vocalization may not be the only significant variable. In their study of speech to 3-month-old Greek children, Roe, Drivas, Karagellis, and Row (1985) reported no difference in the amount of mothers' vocalizations to sons versus daughters. However, the researchers did judge maternal speech to be more affectionate to boys than to girls. The authors correlate this higher level of affection with the finding that the Greek infant males vocalized more than did their female counterparts (a finding at odds with American data).

A curious footnote to these results is that when the authors compared their data with vocalizations by adults to children in a Greek orphanage, the language they observed in the orphanage more closely approximated patterns of vocalization reported in the United States. Baby girls vocalized far more than did their male counterparts. At the same time, the adults' speech addressed to the infant girls was judged more affectionate than speech addressed to boys in the institution and, in fact, more affectionate than the speech natural mothers addressed to their own infant daughters reared at home.

Returning to the United States, we can ask if the phonological profiles of fathers addressing young children differ from those of mothers. Most studies comparing maternal and paternal baby talk have focused on issues of lexicon or syntax, not sound. In my own observations, I have noted two phonologically distinct characteristics of fathers' speech to toddlers. The first is higher *volume*, and the second, an increased *rate* of speaking when communication breaks down (e.g., the child does not respond to the father, or the father fails to understand what the child has said).

Speaking more loudly when comprehension falters is very common among adults who speak different languages but nonetheless need to communicate. To this day, I remember a luncheon 20 years ago, across the street from the Sorbonne, when my monolingual French and American colleagues attempted to shout their way into mutual understanding.

A paternal tendency to increase the rate of speech to toddlers when communication fails is reminiscent of the North Wind (in Aesop's fable) blowing ever harder in an attempt to get the traveller to remove his cloak. Common sense tells us that by speeding up language to a child just learning to talk, we only complicate the task of comprehension. Hence, baby talk typically entails speaking more slowly than to adults. But, attempts to communicate with children are not always governed by logic. Perhaps because of their comparative inexperience in managing young children, many fathers become flustered when they reach a conversational impasse. Quickening the pace of one's speech is a natural response.

The family issue of bilingualism has particularly important phonological ramifications. If you want to raise your child to be bilingual, at what age should you start? Many people argue "the sooner the better." However, researchers agree that while with ample motivation, a speaker can master the grammar and meaning structure of another language at almost any age, native command of the phonology is far more difficult after puberty.

Child-Centered Variables

One of the most important contextual features influencing the phonology of parents' speech is the age of their children. Without a doubt, the average American mother changes the phonological shape of her language as her child goes from infancy to toddlerhood and beyond. (Comparable data on fathers' evolving phonology are not yet available.)

A study by Stern, Spieker, Barnett, and MacKain (1983) illustrates how sharp these maternal shifts can be. The authors examined maternal speech patterns to newborns, 4-month-olds, 12-month-olds, and 24-month olds. Mothers clearly adapted their phonology to the changing needs and abilities of their children. To neonates, who do little but lie on their backs and stare at the passing show, mothers used short vocalizations that were punctuated by long pauses and characterized by relatively bland intonation. By the time the babies were 4 months old, the mothers' phonological patterns began to include a wide range of pitch contours, more varied rhythms, and frequent repetition. The authors argue that because 4-month-olds can sit face-to-face with another person, the mothers' language style was well suited for getting and holding the attention of infants who could easily shift their gaze. By the time children began actively locomoting (between 12 and 24 months), mothers decreased their distinctive baby talk pitch contours and rhythmic variability and began concentrating on longer and more complex utterances better suited to children's evolving linguistic needs.

A second way in which parents respond phonologically to their offspring is "tuning in" to their children's unique pronunciations. We noted in Chapter 3 that as an expression of affection, parents often repeat back their children's less-than-adult pronunciations. Some examples from my own experience include calling bulldozers *bozers*, saying *copersin* for *cooperation*, and injecting an assimilative nasal consonant into the word *truck* when referring to that much loved object, a *dump trunk*.

Does such parental echoing do any harm? No, assuming children have access to correct phonological models (e.g., from *Sesame Street*, other adults, or age-mates). As children learn the correct pronunciation of names for things, they do not hesitate to reject parental mimicry of more immature forms. After several months of my imitating my 2-year-old's pattern of calling a bulldozer a *bozer*, one day my son informed me in no uncertain terms, "Not *bozer*, Ma. *Bulldozer. Bulldozer.*"

6

That's a Pigeon-Bird:
The Growth of Meaning

A common word in many households with young children is *broken*: "Your scooter's broken. We'll need to get it fixed." or "Don't drop that glass. It will get broken." When Aneil was nearly 3, he began using the term in cognate but novel ways. When his aunt fell ill with the flu, the boy announced, "Sheila's broken." The same description went for objects he did not want to encounter (e.g., "My toothbrush is broken"). My favorite use came one morning when we had dropped his father off at work on our way to nursery school. Not happy at his father's departure, Aneil stuck out his lower lip, defiantly pointed to the building his father had just entered, and declared, "Daddy come back. Work is broken."

The question of what a word means in the mind of its user has long fascinated linguists, philosophers, and psychologists. Because most human speech is contextually appropriate, language users often are unaware that their own meaning for a word is at odds with common usage. As a child, I memorized Henry Wadsworth Longfellow's poem, "The Midnight Ride of Paul Revere," that recounts how Revere warned the good citizens of Massachusetts that the British were coming. The line explaining that Revere had ridden "through every Middlesex village and farm" had initially puzzled me, but I deduced that a "middlesex" was probably a small hamlet or town. Only when I attended college in Middlesex County, Massachusetts, did I realize I had parsed the line incorrectly.

Getting a fix on meaning is especially tricky when looking at young children's lexicons. If children use words contextually correctly, we have no double check on their *understanding* of the words' meanings. And of course, we cannot ask a 2- or 3-year-old directly.

WHAT DO WE MEAN BY MEANING?

When we talk about children learning meaning, we really have three interlocking notions in mind. The first aspect of meaning is the words themselves that we use to label objects, actions, and ideas. However, the fact that a child can say a particular word does not guarantee she has the same meaning for it as you do, or even that she has any meaning for it at all. Parents of preschoolers are understandably appalled if their children pick up a term of profanity from older children or adults. But, the good news is that, in most cases, these youngsters have not the vaguest notion what the profane terms mean. A common mistake of language acquisition studies is to draw conclusions about a child's semantic knowledge by considering a list of the words she can say. Such assumptions are irresistible—and irresponsible.

The second component of meaning is the referents of the words themselves. When studying the acquisition of meaning in a child whom you can observe closely (such as your own), you sometimes notice in the course of conversation discrepancies between the standard adult meaning of a word and the way in which the child uses that word. You may find, for example, that your 18-month-old uses *dada* to refer to any adult male, or that your 2-year-old's word *ice cream* refers only to the flavor chocolate.

The third dimension to meaning is sentential context. The meanings of homonyms, for example, only come clear when you hear the surrounding nouns and verbs. Moreover, some aspects of meaning are themselves encoded in syntax, not vocabulary. The *estates general* are very different from *general estates*, and when hearing that "Mary loves Johnny" we cannot infer that "Johnny loves Mary" in return.

In this chapter, we will focus on the first and second aspects of meaning. However, it goes without saying that in the course of modeling sentences, parents shape sentential meaning as well.

SHAPING FIRST WORDS

The appearance of a child's first word around age 1 is an occasion no parent forgets. You revel in the assurance that your child's development is on track, and you relish the boundless possibilities for communication.

What is the first word likely to be? Combining anecdotes with actual studies, the odds-on favorites are some version of names for the parents themselves: *ma* (or *mama*) and *da* (or *dada*). Three notions circulate about why these are likely choices. Common sense suggests that names for parents come early because they are pragmatically so useful. The second option argues that *ma* and *da* are the easiest and most phonologically distinctive sound combinations to make (Jakobson, 1960). A third option, based on a comparison of the phonemes of late babbling with the phonemes of early words, builds the case that phonologically, early words are a continuation of babbling. Data from both American English (e.g., Oller, 1981) and Dutch (e.g., Elbers & Ton, 1985) show that for many children, *da* is the most frequent sound combination in late babbling. Empirically, *da* often appears before *ma* as a first word, lending credence to the third hypothesis.

Aneil's first word, which appeared at about 11.5 months, was *duh*. Its meaning was neither "father" nor "mother," but rather "duck." As I watched this first word emerge, it became clear that a fourth hypothesis was needed to explain early vocabulary: that parents, building upon their children's articulatory propensities, often shape their children's first words, much as a Skinnerian trainer shapes a pigeon or rat.

The day Aneil uttered his first word, we were taking a walk in a nearby park. As I wheeled Aneil in his stroller around to the duck pond, I prattled on as usual:

> It's really hot today, isn't it Aneil? Yeah. Shall we go see the ducks? Here we go down the sidewalk. Look at that big brown duck, Aneil. Do you see it?

Aneil, who had never been much of a babbler, vocalized perfunctorily between my sentential pauses. But, when I reached the end of my spiel, he beamed and said, "Duh."

"Duh?" Like so many other children, Aneil's favorite babble sound was *duh*. He had used it for months as a kind of turn-taking filler. But, as we stood before the ducks, I concluded this was no stray babble, but rather the word *duck*.

Did Aneil really intend to refer to a duck with his "Duh"? I have no way of knowing. What I do know is that I was hungry for real two-way communication, and willing to give the benefit of the doubt to any quasi-linguistic material offered me.

Did Aneil spontaneously say *duck* that day, or did I condition him to associate a babble sound with a meaning? I will never know for sure. I am certain, though, that over the next several years, I consciously taught him words ("That's a cat, Aneil. Can you say *cat*?"). When his initial attempts were off the mark (e.g., *copersin* for *cooperation*), I repeated—and shaped—his sound patterns until he got the words right.

Do all parents shape their children's first words? Probably not. The little girl whose first word was *pretty* (Leopold, 1939-1949) or the little boy whose first word was *turtle* (the son of a friend of mine) probably displayed considerable independence. So, for that matter, do many children whose first word is *ma* or *da*. But, given the understandable desire of parents to communicate with their sons and daughters, the role of parental shaping cannot be ignored.

THE QUESTION OF FREQUENCY

As toddlers become increasingly linguistic during their second and third years of life, what influence do parents have in determining their children's vocabulary? A natural avenue to explore is the frequency of vocabulary words addressed to toddlers: How does adult frequency distribution compare with the order in which words appear in the child's language?

This natural jumping-off point has two immediate problems. First, in assessing children's vocabularies, we must carefully distinguish amongst words children spontaneously utter, words they are capable of uttering, and words they are able to understand. I used to muse that had I done a standard language assessment on my son at age 18 months, he would have shown up quite linguistically retarded. In a typical half hour of free play, he did not utter more than a dozen words. Yet, when we pressed him to respond to picture dictionaries, it was clear that he could name several hundred objects. (His comprehension was even greater.) Aneil's problem was a combination of delayed phonological development and a cautious personality. If he did not know how to say something right, he generally would not volunteer an attempt.

A second problem with a straightforward correlational study of frequency is that the most common words in any adult's lexicon—

the articles *a* and *the*, along with some forms of the verb *to be*—are hardly words you would expect to find in young children's vocabulary. Not only is their meaning opaque, but they are generally unstressed (even buried) in the normal phonological stream.

In their longitudinal study of early grammatical development, Roger Brown and his colleagues (Brown, 1973) asked whether order of language acquisition is predictable from frequency in adult language addressed to children. Brown's data predominantly concerned grammatical endings (e.g., plurals, past tenses, progressive tenses), articles (*a, the*), and prepositions marking location (*in, on*). Brown concluded that frequency of adult usage of these constructions is irrelevant to the order in which children acquire the same grammatical components. Subsequent studies of language acquisition have tended to interpret Brown's finding to mean that frequency of adult usage is never relevant in predicting the path of child language development.

In recent years, common sense has prevailed. Moerk (1980), in a reanalysis of Brown's data, shows that frequency of constructions in adult language does indeed correlate quite closely with order of language acquisition in children. Moreover, whatever the truth regarding obligatory grammatical constructions in adult language, we need to look separately at the question of frequency for basic content words in adult-child conversation. That is, if a father utters the word *dog* five times a day in speaking with his 18-month-old and uses the word *an* five hundred times, we still expect the child to learn *dog* first.

Clearly, the frequency of phonologically salient content words in the speech adults direct to their children generally correlates with the order in which children learn early vocabulary. In the case of more exotic vocabulary such as *puce, cooperation,* or *stegosaurus,* repeated modeling of a word can lead to acquisition of vocabulary far beyond one's years.

Frequent modeling coupled with explanation can also speed children's learning of names for different levels of classification that do not usually appear spontaneously in early language acquisition. Many researchers have noted (e.g., Brown, 1958; Rosch, Mervis, Gray, Johnson, & Boyes-Braem, 1976) that in learning nouns, children tend to acquire names that are neither very specific nor very general before they acquire names at either extreme. In technical parlance, children typically learn basic object categories (e.g., *dog* or *apple*) before superordinates (e.g., *animal* and *fruit*) or subordinates (e.g., *Lhasa apso, golden delicious*).

> BASIC OBJECT: *dog, apple*
> SUPERORDINATE: *animal, fruit*
> SUBORDINATE: *Lhasa apso, golden delicious*

The fact that children generally begin with basic object categories as much reflects the language modeled for them (Blewitt, 1983) as it indicates the practical usefulness of middle-range terms when you have only a small vocabulary. How do children learn nouns at either extreme? Subordinate terms must obviously be modeled by a speaker who knows them (a playmate, a teacher, or a parent).

Superordinate categories are a bit trickier. Not only does the learner need to know the proper word (the first domain of meaning we referred to at the beginning of this chapter) but he also needs to understand which slice of experience the word refers to (our second component of meaning). In the case of basic object or subordinate categories, the matching of word to referent is comparatively easy: You walk past a poodle and say either, "Look at that dog" or "Look at that poodle." The problem with learning superordinate categories is that they are all-encompassing. One would hardly walk down the street, see a poodle approaching, and say to one's 2-year-old, "Look at that animal." Obviously, adults use words like *animal* (e.g., when at the zoo) or *fruit* (when at the grocery store) in the presence of young children, but we do not typically wax pedagogical about them.

Of course, there is no reason why we cannot or should not. One technique I have heard (and used) when at the zoo or when shopping is literally to point up the class relationship between basic object, subordinate, and superordinate categories: "Look at all the fruit over there, Jenny. I see apples, berries, and pears. Those are blueberries. Shall we buy some fruit? What kind of fruit shall we buy?" In writing, this monologue may seem strange, but it is perfectly natural in real-life situations. What's more, it can be highly effective.

Frequent modeling of a word is a useful way to teach class relationships. But, as we will see in a moment, it is not the only one.

WRONG LANGUAGE FOR RIGHT REASONS

For many years, I have been bothered by the methodological assumption in language acquisition studies that children's linguistic progress should be judged against a standard of perfection. Researchers will say, for instance, that children in their study used the past tense 62% of the time it was called for or showed a 91% understanding of the passive voice.

But, wait a minute. If you look at normal adult conversation—language used by speakers who know the system—you do not find perfection. Adults, like children, make mistakes. In fact, in a study I once did of preschoolers' acquisition of syntax, I found that the adult control group scored only 92-95% correct in experiments testing grammatical constructions that I was quite sure they knew (Baron, 1977).

The mistakes adults make in grammar, phonology, or lexicon come about for a variety of reasons. The most common is that we are only human and often "misspeak" ourselves. A second source of incorrect language (mentioned in Chapter 3) is mimicking of children's mistakes as a sign of affection or as a social bridge. But, there is a third—and often conscious—reason that parents use "wrong language." And that is as a form of pedagogy.

Monkey or Chimpanzee?

The most common reason parents use "wrong" vocabulary is to simplify labeling of a complex empirical world. You go to the zoo with your 2-year-old and approach the primate house. Inside are monkeys and gorillas, gibbons and chimpanzees. Let's assume, for the sake of argument, that *you* know the difference between a monkey and a chimpanzee. (It turns out that a large number of college-educated adults do not.) For the past few months, one of the bedtime stories you have been reading is *Curious George*, a delightful book about the adventures of a monkey. Your daughter knows the word *monkey*, but not *chimpanzee*. You approach the first cage, see a chimpanzee, turn to your child, and say—what? A goodly number of us might opt for "Look at the monkey," rather than "Look at the chimpanzee" (see Mervis & Mervis, 1982).

Mislabeling of objects is hardly linguistic child abuse. If adults offered correct and precise labels for everything a child encountered, the child would have a difficult time indeed getting a fix on names and, equally importantly, learning which entities in this world are related to which others. Vultures and hummingbirds have little overt physical resemblance, but by calling them both *birds* we point up their inherent similarities. In much the same way, by labeling all primates *monkeys* (except, of course, *Homo sapiens*, thank you), we indirectly teach children that monkeys, gorillas, gibbons, and chimpanzees somehow all go together. Later, the appropriate linguistic distinctions will follow.

That's a Pigeon-Bird

Given the difficulties children—and adults—have in handling words of classification, it is not surprising that parents invent devices for simplifying this task as well. Let me share with you the method I came up with, and its outcome.

As a student of child language acquisition, I was acutely aware of the problem children have in learning the relationship between different levels of classification. I was especially struck by Jean Piaget's discussion of children who do not yet understand the principle of class inclusion. A child is shown an array of flowers. When asked if there are more Primulas (i.e., primroses) or flowers, the child replies there are more Primulas, failing to understand that Primulas are but one type of flower (Inhelder & Piaget, 1969).

Is there a way to help children avoid this confusion? My own solution emerged one day when my son was about 15 months old. We lived in Washington, D.C., and had decided to spend a Sunday afternoon wandering about the grounds of the Capitol. As any Washington visitor (or resident) knows, the main inhabitants of Capitol Hill are neither politicians nor lobbyists but pigeons.

Aneil was enthralled with his feathered friends. As fast as his wobbly legs would carry him, he chased after first one and then another, hoping to snare a playmate. Aneil generally knew what a bird was from books we had read together and from visitors to our bird feeder at home. But, he had never before seen a pigeon. "Oh Aneil, look at those pigeon-birds," I found myself exclaiming, pairing together a subordinate category with a basic object category. Such terms as *blue-bird*, *butterfish*, and *boxcar* probably suggested the template.

Pigeon-bird was soon followed by *robin-bird* and *sparrow-bird*. Exploring other genuses, I came up with *salmon-fish* and *flounder-fish* (two dinner-time favorites). Other adults in the household quickly joined in.

Correct language modeling? Hardly. But effective? Quite. At age 2, Aneil clearly understood the relationship between *pigeon* and *bird*, *salmon* and *fish*, *rose* and *flower*. In the coming months, he occasionally asked to have *salmon-fish* for dinner, but that locution quickly faded as the adults weaned themselves from such linguistic training wheels.

The Issue of Pronouns

Pronouns pose special problems for children learning language. Unlike nouns, which refer to external objects in the world, pronouns label *relationships* between people. The interlocutor whom I call *you* refers to himself as *I*. A possession I refer to as *mine* my interlocutor needs to call *yours*. Not surprisingly, when children begin learning pronouns, they commonly confuse the terms.

But, is the problem of changing referents the only reason the acquisition of pronouns is comparatively slow? Perhaps not. For when you look carefully at the words parents use to refer to themselves and to their children, you find that the language being modeled is often not standard English.

The first aberration is parental use of proper names in place of pronouns: "Mommy wants Janine to eat her spinach," spoken by an exasperated mother to her 2-year-old. Before I became a parent, I vowed never to engage in such nonsense. To this day, I have unpleasant memories of my second-grade teacher always referring to herself in the third person ("Mrs. Drake wants everyone to sit quietly").

What a difference a child made.

In the first few months after Aneil's birth, my conversations were perfectly grammatical when it came to pronouns: I referred to myself as "I" and to Aneil as "you." However, as his cooing turned to babbling (and soon, I hoped, speech), I found myself slipping into a proper noun mode, "Mommy wants Aneil to go to sleep. Will Aneil please lie down?"

The switch was not conscious, but in retrospect, my motivation was sound. Initially, I sought to teach Aneil to recognize his own name and the names of family members. The next step was for Aneil to produce these names himself. As I have said earlier, Aneil was slow and cautious in his spoken language. When he did pipe up, his words were all monosyllabic: "daddy" was *da*, "truck" was *truh*, "honey" was *hee*, and "Aneil" was *Ah*. I kept up my "wrong language for the right reasons" until the boy could say full versions of his own name and ours. (I assume Mrs. Drake wanted us to remember her name as well.)

Did this strategy noticeably affect other components of Aneil's language acquisition? Yes: He was sharply behind in his development of pronouns. We would get into the car, and Aneil would announce, "Aneil get in Aneil's seat." The child never used *I, me, mine, you,* or *yours.* The good news is that a quick shift in our family language when Aneil was 2;10 yielded rich pronominal fruits. Within days of our consciously switching from proper nouns to appropriate pronouns (and then tossing in some explicit modeling like "You say, `I'm getting in my seat,' " Aneil rapidly began to use pronouns appropriately.

A second aberrant pronominal use common among parents (and lower school teachers) is to substitute the royal *we* for the second person singular pronoun: "Are we ready to brush our teeth and go to bed?" Such ungrammatical use of first person pronouns can serve either as a form of control (especially important in school) or as an expression of affection. The linguistic damage to the child? None, as long as correct pronouns are modeled enough of the time.

Good Night, Allbody

Finally, let us look at whether *children* use wrong language for the right reasons and, if so, whether adults can directly influence such child-generated speech. The usual cases that come to mind are syntactic overgeneralizations—a child saying *goed* instead of *went, mans* instead of *men.* But, the case I want to talk about here is lexical.

One night when he was 2;8, Aneil was heading off to bed with his aunt. A group of family members was gathered around the dining room table. Aneil said goodnight to each of us in turn and then, as his parting farewell, said, "Good night, allbody." This wonderful nonce form is a highly logical blending of *all* (as in "all the people") and the *-body* from *everybody*.

Over the next four months, *allbody* saw much action. Each day when we arrived in the morning at nursery school and the rest of the children were on the playground, Aneil's immediate comment was, "Allbody outside." Each afternoon when we said our farewells, Aneil's parting comment was, "Goodbye, allbody."

Whenever Aneil said *allbody*, I followed with a grammatically correct recast: "That's right, everybody's outside" or "Goodbye, everybody. See you tomorrow." If he responded at all, Aneil's linguistic echo was "Allbody outside," or "Goodbye, allbody." I was perplexed. Here was a child who, at the time, usually repeated every linguistic correction I made. But, when it came to tinkering with a word he had created himself, he proved immune to modeling. At 3;0, Aneil was finally ready for *everybody* and spontaneously began using the word correctly.

MEANING IN CONTEXT
Cultural Customs

As we saw in Chapter 2, societies differ greatly in their views of childhood and notions of appropriate forms of child rearing. In those societies where children are incorporated into the normal flow of life or are treated as low-status individuals (rather than seen as special people needing special care), we would hardly anticipate parents to accommodate their vocabulary to their children's evolving language skills. Ochs (1982), for example, reports that in Western Samoa, where children are seen as lower-status people, caregivers do not use a special baby talk lexicon.

Family Circumstances

In societies such as the United States, in which parental adaptation of language to children is common, what variables determine the kinds of lexical modeling that children receive? Whereas some techniques (such as substitution of first person plural pronouns for the second person singular, or calling all non-human primates *monkeys*) are widespread, other more involuted techniques (e.g., teaching class relationships) are likely to correlate with level of parental education and perhaps parental age.

Another important variable, especially in contemporary middle-class America, is the sex of the parent. While the data are relatively sparse, several studies suggest that at least in traditional households in which the mother is the primary caregiver, mothers tend to use simpler and more common vocabulary than fathers (e.g., Rondal, 1980; Gleason, 1987; Ratner, 1988).

Other researchers have noted that fathers use more specific and semantically correct vocabulary than mothers. Masur and Gleason (1980), using a play task of taking a toy car apart, found that fathers were more likely than mothers to use actual names of car parts or tools (e.g., *wrench*); mothers often resorted to words like *thing*. Ratner (1988) notes that while mothers of children between the ages of 1;6 and 2;0 often substituted "incorrect" labels for objects with which their children were not familiar (e.g., *drum* for *trampoline*, *compass* for *watch*, *ball* for *hockey puck*), fathers of these same children were far more likely to use the correct (though unfamiliar) name.

Such data might be interpreted in one of two ways. On the one hand, we could argue that mothers are especially sensitive to the linguistic level of their children and use age-appropriate words, while fathers (who, at least in these studies, spent relatively little time with their children) are unaware when they are speaking over their child's head. An alternative reading on the data made by Ratner (1988) and others is that whereas mothers essentially play a nurturing role in their children's development, middle-class fathers serve to expand their children's intellectual and experiential horizons.

Looking at the linguistic parenting styles of my own friends and colleagues, I cannot help but wonder to what extent findings from these studies are becoming outmoded. As we enter the 1990s, educated American fathers are taking more interest in and spending more time with their children. At the same time, American women are better educated and have more experience in the professional world outside the home than did women 10 or 15 years ago.

A third important factor is the overwhelming success of television's *Sesame Street*, which uses a surprisingly sophisticated vocabulary in programming now regularly viewed by children at least as young as 12 months. *Sesame Street* has upped the linguistic ante for parents of either sex. If current trends continue, vocabulary used by middle-class mothers and fathers to their children may well become increasingly similar, and words from both parents become increasingly complex.

Child-Centered Variables

What about the effects the child himself or herself has on a parent's modeling of vocabulary? I leave you with two pieces of advice.

First, parents can be most helpful in modeling new words if they focus on activities and objects their children care about. Naming all the flowers in your garden is probably a waste of time if your daughter is preoccupied with wood working or painting. Parents should not hesitate to introduce words—even complex words— that are appropriate to the situation that captures a child's interest. A 3-year-old fixated on dinosaurs can master such names as *triceratops*, *diplodocus*, and *ankylosaurus* even more quickly than her parents.

Second, you need not feel guilty about mirroring your child's nonce forms as an expression of affection or as an avenue for social exchange. Many children make up their own labels for things or people, often because they cannot pronounce the real word or do not happen to know an object's name. On occasion, these invented words stick forever (e.g., children's names for siblings or for family pets). Most likely, though, especially in the case of common nouns, the child will eventually switch to the community norm.

When one little boy was 13 months old, his family happened upon a fountain shaped like a giant water faucet. At this stage, the child understood the word *water*, but was nowhere near being able to pronounce a polysyllabic word, especially one beginning with a *w* (a very difficult sound to articulate). Entranced by the fountain, the toddler spontaneously proclaimed, "ish," imitating the sound of the falling water.

From then onward, the boy used *ish* to label everything involving water: water from the tap, fire hydrants, hoses, lawn sprinklers. Charmed, his family followed suit: "Would you like a glass of ish?" or "Look at the green ish stretched out on that lawn."

The good news, of course, is that the child was also exposed to the

words *water, fire hydrant, hose,* and *sprinkler* from other sources—
books, television, school teachers, and playmates. Gradually, the
boy began using the word *water,* and soon the other standard words
began to follow as well.

7

Would You Like Some Up? : Parents and Grammar

Language and politics are inextricably connected. From Ireland to India, Belgium to the Basque country, populations have linked their ethnic identity to the issue of national language.

The emergence of a new political grouping often has linguistic consequences. The return of Jews from across Europe to Palestine in the early 1900s, the Chinese revolution of the 1940s, and the 1917 Russian Revolution all included concerted efforts to acculturate diverse ethnic populations into one language community.

The case of the Soviet Union is particularly interesting because the politically motivated directive for all ethnic populations to learn Russian became a research goal of Soviet psychologists interested in the relationship between language, cognition, and socialization (see Wertsch, 1985). Psychologists such as Lev Vygotsky argued that the development of both cognitive and linguistic skills could be enhanced through appropriate instruction. By the 1940s, a research tradition had begun to emerge grounded on the premise that young children's acquisition of grammar can be accelerated through pedagogy, assuming the child is at a stage in his development where such pedagogy can take hold (e.g., no one was suggesting teaching tense markers to 12-month-olds).

In the experiments stemming from this tradition, teaching took various forms. In some studies (e.g., Popova, 1973), the experimenters directly corrected children's ungrammatical utterances, such as, putting the correct marker of grammatical gender on the end of a noun. In other investigations (e.g., Bogoyavlenskiy, 1973), experimenters talked with children about the components of a word so that youngsters came to understand how a root word like *white* gets paired with a suffix like *-ness* (the goal being to teach children the productive use of grammatical inflections).

In the United States, attitudes toward language acquisition and teaching have always been markedly distinct. Although we have, from the beginning, been a polyglot nation, the population itself has largely borne the responsibility for learning English. Children of immigrants learned English from friends or in school, not because they were treated to special pedagogies (federally-funded bilingual programs are very recent in America), but because this was the way to survive and prosper. Noam Chomsky's later insistence that language cannot be taught meshed both with already established American attitudes toward language acquisition and with practical realities. To this day, many immigrant parents do not themselves know English (or know it well).

The nature-nurture debate between Chomsky and Skinner did not begin as a battle over pedagogy in early language acquisition. At the time (the late 1950s), behaviorists, including Skinner, knew very little about human language acquisition, and Chomsky's experience was just as sparse. The intellectual exchange had more to do with conflicting assumptions about the character of the human mind and its capacity to think and learn. Yet, over the years, the arguments posed on both sides have focused on language acquisition, and, in particular, on the acquisition of grammar.

The reason that grammar—not conversation, not phonology, and not lexicon—has dominated the debate is that grammar, much more than the other areas of language, is open-ended. The conventions of conversation are well established. The number of phonemes (and phonemic combinations) in a language is set. Relatively few new words appear in a language from year to year. But, the number of new phrases and sentences is potentially infinite. Because children cannot have heard all the sentences they will some day utter, Chomsky took grammar as the logical proving ground for his position in the nature-nurture controversy.

Through most of the 1960s and the early 1970s, researchers interested in language acquisition focused considerable attention on the development of grammar in young children. Overwhelmingly, they presupposed a Chomskyan perspective. However well-meaning and "objective" their research techniques, their studies continued to feed the theory that grammar essentially emerges from the child, and that parents can do little to affect the process.

By the mid 1970s, a growing number of linguists and psychologists had become increasingly interested in the social dynamics of language acquisition: the acquisition of conversational skills, the interaction between child and parent, and even the possible influence of parental speech on children's developing language. By the end of the 1980s, a sizable literature had emerged examining the question of whether parents do (or can) influence the course of their children's acquisition of grammar.

Most of the discussion has grown out of an initial debate over the role of baby talk in language acquisition. In 1977, Catherine Snow and Charles Ferguson published the proceedings of a 1974 conference entitled "Language Input and Acquisition" (Snow & Ferguson, 1977). The volume constituted the first extensive discussion of baby talk, including a pivotal article by Elissa Newport, Henry Gleitman, and Lila Gleitman entitled "Mother, I'd Rather Do It Myself: Some Effects and Non-Effects of Maternal Speech Style" (Newport, Gleitman, & Gleitman, 1977). Katherine Nelson and her colleagues provided the most pointed response to Newport et al. (Furrow, Nelson, & Benedict, 1979), with a full-fledged debate unfolding over the next decade (e.g., Gleitman, Newport, & Gleitman, 1984; Furrow & Nelson, 1986). Whereas Newport and her colleagues maintained that the use of baby talk is largely irrelevant to children's emerging grammar, Nelson and her group argued for a more positive role.

Who is right?

CAN GRAMMAR BE TAUGHT? THE DATA
On Proving Causation

These days, no one questions that most American parents in some way modify the language they address to children. While it is difficult to know how to measure the effects of such baby talk when it functions as a means of control, affection, and social exchange, it is natural to look for ways of assessing the pedagogical effects of parental language.

The measurement question is especially tricky when it comes to grammar acquisition. Unlike the domains of phonology and lexicon, most of the grammatical manifestations of baby talk are not expressed by special forms of language (compare, e.g., the use of higher pitch or lexical substitutions). As a result, many parents are unaware that they are engaging in the use of grammatically-driven baby talk. Moreover, because manifestations of baby talk in grammar are often subtle, the effects may not show up immediately and, when they do, they sometimes appear in a different realm of grammar.

Most studies of the possible effects of adult grammar on children's developing language take samples from two points in time and look for possible relationships. The language of both parent and child is sampled at time T_1, and then another sample is taken again at time T_2. If a correlation (positive or negative) appears between the parent's use of baby talk features at T_1 and grammatical development in the child's language between T_1 and T_2, the study concludes a causal relationship between parental use of baby talk and the child's grammar acquisition.

A neat package, but one frought with problems.

Even in the simplest of cases (e.g., frequent parental use of the passive voice correlating with early acquisition of passives by the child), we cannot necessarily conclude that the parental speech pattern *causes* the child's linguistic development, because children hear passives from other sources as well (e.g., television, nursery school teachers, other adults). Cases involving indirect relationships are more delicate still. For example, we will see in a moment that frequent use of *yes/no* questions by adults tends to correlate with the development of auxiliary verbs. Actually *proving* that adult modeling of sentence types that happen to contain auxiliaries caused the children's acquisition of auxiliaries is yet another matter.

For as any beginning student of philosophy knows, correlation must not be confused with causation. High cholesterol levels correlate with heart disease, but we now suspect the major culprits are actually fat intake and lack of exercise. Even the strength of correlation between two events has no bearing on the likelihood of a causal relationship. American interest in foreign foods has coincided with the growth of acid rain, yet we hardly suggest a causal connection. Much the same way, we cannot conclude that because a parent's frequent use of a particular construction type correlates with her child's acquisition of another linguistic construction, that one caused the other.

We need, then, to ponder how to evaluate correlations we find. My advisor in graduate school, Charles Ferguson, often warned me to use statistics very cautiously in studying language acquisition. He used to say that if you cannot see a relationship by looking at the raw data, think long and hard before believing what your correlations tell you.

Another problem with interpreting existing correlational studies of parental language and child acquisition is that we are often comparing apples and oranges. The age of children investigated varies from study to study. A discrepancy in results between two studies (one of which used 2-year-old subjects and the other of which used 3-year-olds) may really be telling us not that the findings disagree, but that the effect of parents on children's language varies with the child's level of development. To complicate matters further, not all studies compare change in children's grammar from time T_1 to time T_2. Some simply correlate adult usage at T_1 with child usage at T_1.

Having donned our cautionary life jackets, let us see what correlations we are talking about.

Types of Teaching

As we consider specific constructions and styles of grammar used by parents, it will be helpful to cluster the data into related categories. Therefore, we will look first at *grammar-specific issues* (involving particular grammatical constructions adults use in talking with their children), and then turn to *conversation issues* (that is, grammatical components of discourse styles used by adults that potentially lead to grammatical growth in their children's language).

Grammar-Specific Issues

In reviewing the existing literature on the effects of parental language on children's developing grammar, we find that four syntactic parameters have received the most attention: sentence length, the occurrence of imperatives, the use of questions, and overall sentential complexity. Often these parameters overlap.

We begin with the question of length. In their comparative study of children at age 1;6 and then again at 2;3, Furrow, Nelson, and

Benedict (1979) report changing correlations over time between maternal MLU (mean length of utterance) and growth of children's MLU. Shorter maternal MLUs when the children were 1;6 (and had an average MLU of 1) predicted more rapid growth of the children's MLU nine months later. However, looking at maternal speech when the same children were 2;3, the study found that longer maternal MLUs correlated positively with longer MLUs in their children. The authors argue that the initially shorter maternal MLU is instrumental in clearly laying out syntactic relationships, while the longer MLUs directed to older children (who had, by then, embarked upon syntax) provide a rich syntactic model that stimulates syntactic growth.

Not all researchers agree with Furrow et al.'s findings. Barnes, Gutfreund, Satterly, and Wells (1983) found no correlation between mothers' average sentence length and their children's syntactic development. (We note that children in the Barnes et al. study already had average MLUs of 1.5.)

In talking about sentence length, we need to remember that sentences can be short for a variety of reasons. Sometimes only a limited number of grammatical relations are being expressed (e.g., "Billie saw the dog" or "The milk spilled"). But in other instances, imperatives—which are shorter than declaratives or interrogatives—are dominating the mother's side of the conversation.

Several investigators report a negative effect of maternal imperatives upon children's syntactic development. Gleitman, Newport, and Gleitman (1984), for example, note a negative correlation between maternal imperatives and children's growth of auxiliaries and of noun inflections. McDonald (1979) hypothesizes that mothers who use a sizable number of imperatives tend to dominate conversations rather than encouraging children to vocalize.

As in the case of sentence length, however, we should not be overly hasty in assuming that all imperatives are conceptually and functionally equal. There is a vast difference between an imperative like "Stop it!" and an imperative such as "Please help me put all the blocks back into the bag." While the first type of imperative is unlikely to encourage language development (i.e., other than of imperatives), the second sort might well be useful. In fact, Furrow, Nelson, and Benedict (1979) report a *positive* correlation between mothers' use of imperatives and their children's syntactic development for samples of mother and child speech taken when the children were 2;3. Significant correlations are reported between maternal use of imperatives and the children's growing MLU, number of verbs per utterance, and number of noun phrases per utterance. Discrepancies between Gleitman, Newport, and Gleitman (1984) and Furrow et al. may reflect the vagaries of experimental correlational studies. To be certain, it would help to have a fine-grained analysis of the *content* of the imperatives at issue.

Mothers' use of questions is probably the richest source of data currently available on the influence of parents' speech on children's syntactic development. Starting with *yes/no* questions (e.g., "Are you drawing a spider?"), we find unilateral agreement among researchers (e.g., Newport, Gleitman, & Gleitman, 1977; Furrow, Nelson, & Benedict, 1979; Barnes, Gutfreund, Satterly, & Wells, 1983) that the asking of *yes/no* questions positively correlates with syntactic development in children, especially in the acquisition of auxiliaries (such as the *are* in "Are you drawing a spider?"). The reason is fairly clear. By placing the auxiliary first in the sentence, the mother highlights the construction both phonologically and syntactically. We must point out, however, that the pedagogical effectiveness of *yes/no* questions on syntactic development may be limited in scope. Studies by Hoff-Ginsberg and her colleagues (Hoff-Ginsberg & Shatz, 1982; Hoff-Ginsberg, 1985) indicate that by the time children reach age 2, their acquisition of auxiliaries is more closely linked to maternal use of auxiliaries in general and to use of *wh*-questions than to *yes/no* questions.

While *yes/no* questions only call for the child to agree or disagree, *wh*- questions (i.e., *who, what, where, why, when,* and *how*) require children to respond with a specific word or phrase. Not surprisingly, children learn to respond appropriately to *yes/no* questions before they can handle *wh*- questions.

Parental use of *wh*- questions seems to correlate positively with children's language development. Studying children between the ages of 2;0 and 2;6, Hoff-Ginsberg (1986) observes that maternal use of *wh*- questions is positively correlated with children's subsequent development of verbs and later, of auxiliaries. Note, however, that not all *wh*- questions figure equally in maternal speech to young children. As Ervin-Tripp and Miller (1977) have commented, certain *wh*- questions (particularly *why*, *when*, and *how*) are semantically more complex than others (i.e., *who, what*, and *where*). Not surprisingly, parents of young children tend to avoid the more complex *wh*-questions or at least not to expect answers to them.

Other question types have also been shown to predict language development. Mothers' tag questions (e.g., "You're a little sleepy, aren't you?") correlate positively with young children's MLU (Furrow, Nelson, & Benedict, 1979). At the same time, test questions (i.e., questions whose answers you are certain the child already knows) may *negatively* correlate with some measures of syntactic growth (Yoder & Kaiser, 1989).

While other specific areas of grammar bear investigation (see, for example, Hoff-Ginsberg, 1986, for data on noun acquisition; Gleitman, Newport, & Gleitman, 1984, for the impact of maternal use of deictic terms and utterances [e.g., "Here is the milk" "That's a ball"] on children's development of nominal inflections), a more global question is how the overall complexity of a mother's utterances relates to children's emerging grammar. What do we mean by *complexity*? While no uniform definition is adopted in the literature, the notion of complexity is typically associated with longer sentences on the one hand and use of words without transparent referents or syntactic meaning on the other. For example, Furrow, Nelson, and Benedict (1979) define complex utterances as entailing longer length, pronouns in lieu of nouns, and verbs in lieu of nouns, copulas, or contractions.

Not surprisingly, researchers roundly disagree on the efficacy of using simpler versus more complex syntax as a means of stimulating children's syntactic growth. Barnes, Gutfreund, Satterly, and Wells (1983) report no correlation between adult complexity and children's syntactic progress. In their original study, Newport, Gleitman, and Gleitman (1977) conclude that

> [w]hether mothers speak in long sentences or short ones, restricted or wide-ranging sentence types, complex sentences or simple ones—none of these plausible candidates for a teaching style have a discernible effect on the children's language growth during the six month interval we investigated. (p.136)

In a later reanalysis of their original data, Gleitman, Newport, and Gleitman (1984) argue that greater maternal complexity positively correlates with children's language development. Yet, Furrow, Nelson, and Benedict (1979) strongly maintain that complexity *hampers* syntactic development:

> those aspects of motherese which reflect the use of a simpler communication style were positively related to language growth while the use of a more complex style was associated with relatively slower child language development. (p.436)

A definitive resolution of the debate does not seem immediately forthcoming. Researchers' methods of data collection and data analysis are not sufficiently homogeneous, and sample sizes are still too small to allow proper comparison or to factor out individual variation in language learning patterns. Nonetheless, two important dimensions have surfaced as potential sources of explanation for the current discrepancies.

The first of these variables is the age of the child. Furrow, Nelson, and Benedict (1979) found dramatic differences between (1) correlations between maternal speech when children were 1;6 and children's speech at 2;3, and (2) correlations between maternal speech when children were 2;3 and children's speech at the same age. Under the first condition, the authors report the following significant correlations.

POSITIVE CORRELATIONS
Mother: total *yes/no* questions   *Child*: auxiliaries per verb phrase
Mother: non-inverted *yes/no* questions   *Child*: MLU

NEGATIVE CORRELATIONS
Mother: pronouns   *Child*: verbs per utterance
Mother: verbs   *Child*: verbs per utterance
Mother: contractions   *Child*: noun phrases per utterance
Mother: copulas   *Child*: MLU
                          verbs per utterance
                          noun phrases per utterance

Correlations—both positive and negative—under the second

condition are entirely different.

POSITIVE CORRELATIONS

Mother: imperatives	*Child*: MLU
	verbs per utterance
	noun phrases per utterance
Mother: verbs	*Child*: MLU
	verbs per utterance
	noun phrases per utterance

NEGATIVE CORRELATIONS

Mother: interjections	*Child*: MLU
	verbs per utterance
	noun phrases per utterance

(Furrow, Nelson, & Benedict, 1979, pp. 433-434)

This crazy quilt of findings may, as Gleitman, Newport, and Gleitman (1984) suggest, actually be no findings at all. Alternatively, if replicable, the data may indicate that the role of parents in children's acquisition of syntax is highly linked to the child's stage of development. Even Gleitman et al. conclude that while parental input has little influence on later child language development, parents may be instrumental in helping shape the syntax of very young children.

If the child's age is one possible explanation for the divergent results we have seen, then persistent adult modeling of syntax in the normal course of conversational exchange is another. A growing number of studies (e.g., Nelson, Carskaddon, & Bonvillian, 1973; Nelson, 1977; Baker & Nelson, 1984; Roth, 1984; Schwartz, Chapman, Prelock, Terrell, & Rowan, 1985) have demonstrated that explicit modeling of syntax not yet used by children correlates with subsequent acquisition of those constructions. Such modeling by adults in the form of recasts of prior utterances by the child seems to be especially useful in fostering syntax acquisition. (See, in particular, the work of K. E. Nelson and his colleagues.)

Adult recasts are but one of the conversational forms of baby talk. We turn now to these parental conversational techniques to see what influence they have upon children's emerging grammar.

Conversation Issues

We begin with parents' use of repetitions—either self-repetitions or repetitions of their child's utterance. Hoff-Ginsberg (1985, 1986) reports that maternal self-repetitions (or partial self-repetitions) in conversation with children between 2;0 and 2;6 correlate with subsequent child development of verbs. With regard to maternal repetition of a child's preceding utterance, Hoff-Ginsberg (1985) finds that under certain conditions, partial repetitions of the child's earlier sentence correlate with the child's subsequent development of noun phrase complexity.

What about expansions—again, either of the parent's own utterances or of the child's? Cross (1978) notes a positive correlation between mothers' expansions of their own prior utterances and their children's subsequent grammatical development. A number of researchers (including Newport, Gleitman, & Gleitman, 1977; Barnes, Gutfreund, Satterly, & Wells, 1983; and Hoff-Ginsberg, 1985) report that expansions of children's utterances seem to contribute to their development of such syntactic dimensions as MLU, auxiliaries, and noun phrase complexity.

These contemporary—and consistent—findings on the positive effects of expanding children's utterances directly contradict an early study by Cazden (1965) that concluded adult expansions have no facilitating effect upon children's subsequent acquisition of syntax. The Cazden study has played a particularly important role in the language acquisition literature. For over two decades, her research has repeatedly been cited as evidence that parents have little, if any, influence upon children's acquisition of language. Only recently have students of language acquisition recognized that Cazden's research—involving a highly artificial experimental setting in which preschoolers received 40 minutes daily of adult expansions of their utterances—is not relevant to natural conversational give-and-take between parent and child.

Besides repetitions and expansions, parents often recast their children's previous utterances, drawing upon the child's own vocabulary or syntax to continue conversation. A spectrum of studies (including Brown, 1958; Moerk, 1972; Nelson, Furrow, & Benedict, 1979; Baker & Nelson, 1984; Hoff-Ginsberg, 1985) indicates that recasts are a valuable tool in the acquisition of syntax. It seems likely that constructions that maintain some (but not all) of the structure and content of a previous utterance provide the developing child an especially clear source for subsequent linguistic growth.

Another conversational issue involves parents' responses to children's ungrammatical utterances. In 1970, Brown and Hanlon stated categorically that "there [is not] even a shred of evidence that approval and disapproval [by parents of a child's utterances] are contingent on syntactic correctness" (p.47). As we saw in Chapter 1, this position led language acquisition researchers for many years to assume that children's grammaticality is irrelevant to the way in which their parents interact with them linguistically.

In recent years, our notions of "relevance" have become more sophisticated. While most parents do not directly comment upon the grammaticality of their children's utterances, a growing body of research suggests that parents nonetheless are aware of whether or not these utterances are grammatical when formulating conversational responses. Studying the speech of mothers to their 2-year-olds, Hirsch-Pasek, Treiman, and Schneiderman (1984) found that mothers were more likely to repeat (and, *en passant*, to correct) their children's ungrammatical utterances than their grammatical sentences. Again looking at 2-year-olds, Demetras, Post, and Snow (1986) observed that the nature of mothers' repetitions depended upon the grammaticality of their children's utterances: Mothers tended to use more exact repetitions and "move-ons" (i.e., responses continuing the conversation without either questioning or repeating the child's previous utterance) following well-formed utterances, and to use more extended or contracted repetitions (i.e., either longer or shorter than the child's original utterance) following ill-formed utterances. In the same vein, Penner (1987), studying children with MLUs between 2.0 and 3.5, concluded that parents (especially when addressing linguistically less advanced children) were more likely to expand children's ungrammatical utterances and to extend the topic following grammatical utterances.

GRAMMAR TEACHING AND COMMON SENSE

Taken as a group, the studies we have been reviewing clearly indicate both that parents take note of their children's linguistic form and content, and that parental language has demonstrable effects upon children's subsequent development of grammar. Just what are these effects and why do they occur? Until we have identified all the relevant variables, it is hard to be sure. In the meanwhile, though, common sense suggests some reasonable paths through the data maze.

To begin, we can reiterate our warning about not confusing correlation with causation. The temptation to read significance into a correlation merely because it supports your theory must be resisted. The sheer number of conflicting correlations we have encountered in this section should help bolster our resolve. So should correlations that make no sense or are blatantly counterintuitive. Commenting on results reported by Furrow, Nelson, and Benedict (1979), Gleitman, Newport, and Gleitman (1984) observe that

> [Furrow et al.] found that mothers who used more copulas and more contractions to their offspring had children who came to say fewer noun-phrases per utterance than the offspring of mothers who used fewer copulas or contractions. If such an effect is real, what could be its explanation? (p.51)

Even more pointedly, Gleitman et al. note the absurdity of their own finding of a "POSITIVE, 0.99 correlation between maternal UNINTELLIGIBILITY and child growth in verbs per utterance, in the younger age group" (p.64).

Second, we have seen that the child's age (and stage of linguistic development) is probably a crucial factor in determining influence of parental modeling on children's grammar acquisition. While Gleitman, Newport, and Gleitman (1984) may or may not be correct that parental influence is only significant with younger children, it is clear that the influence of parental language alters over time.

Third, a great deal of work remains to be done in identifying the right syntactic variables for comparison, both in adult and child speech. One move is to make analysis of syntactic structure finer-grained. Hoff-Ginsberg (1986), for example, speaks not of "questions" but of real questions, verbal reflective questions, action reflective questions, repair questions, test questions, report questions, and prompts. Similarly, in referring to mothers' self-repetitions, Hoff-Ginsberg (1985) distinguishes amongst at least 11 varieties.

Another dimension of the syntactic variable issue is the clustering of parental linguistic behaviors. Olsen-Fulero (1982), McDonald and Pien (1982), Yoder and Kaiser (1989), and others distinguish between a *conversation-eliciting style* and a *conversation-directing style*. The former tends to be filled with requests for information from the child, while the latter contains imperatives or test questions (i.e., the answers to which are already determined). By and large, a conversation-eliciting style correlates with children's syntactic development and a conversation-directing style predicts slower linguistic growth.

An alternative way of looking at the issue of how variables cluster is to see whether parents balance simplicity in one part of their language modeling with complexity in another. For example, parents might mix simple syntax with more complex vocabulary (e.g., "Here is some scrumptious spinach") or complex syntax with heavy emphasis on important words (e.g., "That *face* hasn't been *washed* all day").

In looking at how common sense can help us identify appropriate variables concerning parental influence on children's learning of syntax, we have focused so far on methodological themes (i.e., the dangers of correlational studies, the significance of age, and the clustering of variables). Let us now turn to the role of broader contextual issues.

GRAMMAR IN CONTEXT
Cultural Customs

The kinds of grammatical modeling we have been discussing thus far are all characteristic of the language that contemporary middle-class American parents use with toddlers and preschoolers. In this cultural milieu, parents typically devote considerable effort to nurturing their children's linguistic development and, more generally, to interacting with and accommodating to their offsprings' behavior. In addition to using repetitions, expansions, and recasts, for example, parents often construct ungrammatical utterances or incorporate children's ungrammatical language into their own (see

Chapter 2). Thus, it is not uncommon to find American parents asking such questions as "Do you have a hurt?" or "Would you like some up?"

The syntactic choices parents make in constructing conversations with their children are heavily dependent upon how the broader culture defines appropriate roles for parents and children. In the United States, accommodation to young children (and their language) is commonplace. Conventions in other societies are often starkly different. For example, in both Guatemala (Pye, 1986) and New Guinea (Schieffelin, 1979), adults rarely imitate what their children say. Ochs (1982) reports that in Western Samoa, parents do not expand their children's utterances. Ochs explains that the absence of such expansions by Samoan caregivers derives from their cultural assumption that children must learn to adjust to the perspective of adults, not vice versa.

Family Circumstances

Turning from the broader culture to the family, we find a growing wealth of studies focusing upon questions of grammar and gender: Does the sex of the parent—or the child—influence the kind of grammar adults address to children, and, if so, how do such differences affect children's grammatical development?

In earlier chapters, we noted a handful of sex-related differences in the realms of conversation, phonology, and lexicon. However, grammar is the area in which most of the research on sex differences in language modeling is being done. What is more, grammar turns out to be particularly important both because of its far-reaching impact and because of its subtlety. The grammatical adjustments parents make in their speech to children are less evident to the casual observer than, say, pitch level or sophistication of vocabulary. As a result, parents tend to be unaware of differences in their linguistic input to sons versus daughters.

The data prove as elusive as the phenomenon. Several studies (e.g., Golinkoff & Ames, 1979; Hladik & Edwards, 1984; Kavanaugh & Jirkovsky, 1982) have concluded that overall, sex of parent or child does not affect the grammatical style of language that adults address to children. However, when we look at specific grammatical issues (and at the findings of other researchers), the story quickly becomes more complex.

Begin with an objective measure like the average length of parents' utterances to young children. While Golinkoff and Ames (1979) found no differences in the length of utterances mothers and fathers addressed to their 19-month-old babies, a host of researchers (e.g., Gleason, 1987; Malone & Guy, 1982; McLaughlin, White, McDevitt, & Raskin, 1983; Hladik & Edwards, 1984; Weintraub, 1977) report that the average length of fathers' utterances to their children was shorter than that of mothers' utterances to children. (NOTE: Children in these studies ranged in age from 1;6—that is, about the age of toddlers in the Golinkoff & Ames study—to 4;4.) At the same time, Cherry and Lewis (1976) note that the average utterance length of mothers to their 2-year-old daughters was longer than that of mothers to their 2-year-old sons.

Why does maleness (of parent or child) seem to correlate with shorter utterances? A probable explanation is that so many sentences addressed by fathers and to sons are imperatives ("Don't do that!", "Stop!", etc.), and imperatives take less verbal space than declaratives conveying the same meaning (e.g., "I wish you would stop doing that"). Comparing the number of imperatives that mothers and fathers address to their children, we find that fathers tend to use far more imperatives than mothers. Malone and Guy (1982) report that fathers used three times as many imperatives as mothers to 3-year-old sons, and Gleason (1987) found that in the language fathers used at home to their sons, fully 38% of all utterances were imperatives. (The percentage dropped somewhat when the same fathers spoke with their sons under laboratory conditions.) What is more, Bellinger and Gleason (1982) confirm that while fathers tend to express requests through direct imperative constructions (e.g., "Turn that bolt"), mothers are more likely to articulate requests through questions (e.g., "Could you turn that bolt?").

Data on the use of imperatives to male and female children confirm the association of direct imperatives with maleness. Weintraub (1977), and Cherry and Lewis (1976) observe that mothers of boys are more likely to use imperatives than are mothers of girls. Bellinger and Gleason (1982) note that by the time their subjects were 4 years old, the children's own use of directives (e.g., imperatives versus questions) mirrored that of their same-sex parents.

Adults' use of questions to children is an important domain for examining the role of sex-linked modeling in language development. Because an interrogative invites an answer, our questions to children (rhetorical or test questions aside) encourage verbalization, which in turn stimulates language development. Moreover, the kinds of questions we ask influence the kinds of language development we encourage. *Yes/no* questions (e.g., "Have you been eating some cake?") nurture the acquisition of auxiliary verbs, while *wh-* questions (e.g., "What is the name of your dog?" or "Who is sitting on your lap?") require a higher level of grammatical sophistication to answer correctly.

The data on sex differences in parents' questions to young children are all over the map. Given the number of variables we need to control for (sex of parent, sex of child, age of child, type of question asked), it is hardly surprising that existing studies provide only glimpses of the larger phenomenon. For example, while Cherry and Lewis (1976) note that mothers ask more questions of their 2-year-old daughters than of their 2-year-old sons, McLaughlin, White, McDevitt, and Raskin (1983) conclude that mothers ask more questions of children of either sex than do fathers. Weintraub (1977) reports that mothers ask more questions of sons, and fathers more questions of daughters. Weintraub further observes that mothers and fathers alike ask more *yes/no* questions than *wh-* questions of their 3- and 4-year-old daughters. And so it goes.

Turning from grammar-specific to conversational issues, we find scattered evidence of sex-related differences in parental speech to children. McLaughlin et al. (1983) found that fathers repeated their own utterances to sons and daughters (from age 1;6 to 3;6) more often than did mothers. Rondal (1980), observing children from 1;6 to 3;0, noted that mothers were more likely to correct their children's speech than were fathers. In their study of mothers' speech to 2-year-olds, Cherry and Lewis (1976) reported that mothers repeated their daughters' utterances more often than their sons'.

Taken together, all of these studies would seem to indicate that grammatically, mothers take a more active—and interactive—role with their children than do fathers, and that mothers are especially linguistically demanding of their daughters. If these tendencies do, in fact, exist, parents of both sexes may be well advised to monitor their differential behaviors if they are to maximize the pedagogical effectiveness of linguistic exchanges with their children.

Child-Centered Variables

Despite all the familial pressures that help mold children's acquisition of grammar, we must not overlook the counterbalancing role of children as individuals. Since Katherine Nelson's seminal work distinguishes between referential and expressive styles in children's early vocabulary acquisition (Nelson, 1973), a growing number of researchers have been grappling with such questions as where these differences come from, how individual variation manifests itself across the different components of language (i.e., in phonology, lexicon, syntax, and conversation), and how this variation relates to the language adults model for children. (See, for example, Wells, 1986, for a review of the literature, and Nelson, 1981; Furrow & Nelson, 1984; and Speidel & Nelson, 1989, for more focused studies.)

In light of our interest in the role of parents in helping shape children's acquisition of grammar, relevant questions about variation in learning styles include the following:

Are differences in children's learning styles the cause or the result of differences in the ways parents converse with children?

What happens when there is a "mismatch" between a child's learning style and his parents' conversational style?

How are particular learning styles affected by specific aspects of parents' conversation?

A number of studies (e.g., Nelson, 1973; Della Corte, Benedict, & Klein, 1983; Furrow & Nelson, 1984) have noted correlations between children's early language acquisition patterns and parents' conversational style. While parents obviously play an important role in shaping their children's approach to language (as evidenced by robust differences between acquisition patterns in first and second children—see Nelson, 1973), many researchers have argued that at least in the early stages of acquisition, it is often the child, not the parent, who establishes conversational patterns (e.g., Smolak & Weinraub, 1983; Murray & Trevarthen, 1986; Smolak, 1987).

How important is it that children and their parents share conversational styles? Following Nelson's (1973) initial observations about behavioral tensions she observed when expressive children were "mismatched" with referential parents (and vice versa), a number of researchers have noted that language acquisition is facilitated when parents and children share approaches to discourse (see, for example, Nelson, Baker, Denninger, Bonvillian, & Kaplan, 1985; Lieven, 1978, 1984).

As yet, relatively little is known about the interaction between children's later learning styles and the language modeled for them by parents. Several researchers (e.g., Nelson, 1981; Nelson, Denninger, Bonvillian, Kaplan, & Baker, 1984; Speidel, 1987) have suggested that exact imitations by parents of children's utterances may hamper the child's rate of grammar acquisition. To understand the import of such findings, we will need, for example, to determine whether some children benefit from hearing—and from producing—imitations more than others (see Speidel & Nelson, 1989).

8

Expanded Conversations: Reading and Television

So far, we have been looking at the potential effects of parental face-to-face conversation on children's emerging spoken language abilities. In this chapter, we expand the discussion to examine how the interaction children have with two other media—writing and television—shape their emerging language skills. Our discussion of literacy focuses less on the skills themselves than on the mediating role parents can play in the acquisition process. Our analysis of television looks at "conversations" between child, characters on screen, and parents.

Why cluster early literacy with television viewing? Pragmatically, since the appearance of quality children's television programming in the late 1960s, the context in which the average American child learns the rudiments of reading has shifted from a strictly "between two covers" activity to a multimedia event involving both hard copy and moving images.

From a theoretical perspective, both reading and television involve visual experiences (in contrast with the spoken word). Visual information tends to be processed—and remembered—differently from auditory information. For example, in a study of third and sixth graders' comprehension and memory of information conveyed through television, writing, or radio, Pezdek, Lehrer, and Simon (1984) report comparable levels of performance on the television and reading tasks, and inferior memory for the radio condition.

Similarly, Swiss researchers (Sturm & Jorg, 1981) have shown that when kindergarten and first grade children see a story on television or hear it on the radio, they are more successful at solving spatial problems based on the story when the information has been presented on television.

Let us look, in turn, at children's early experience with reading and with television, and then see how the two connect.

EMERGENT LITERACY: THE PRINCIPLES

What is the best way to teach children to read? About the only conclusion educators share is that children should never be forced into literacy—whether at age 3 or at age 6 or 7. Beyond this truism, we find wide diversity on the question of method. While Glenn Doman (author of *How to Teach Your Baby to Read* and founder of the Better Baby Institute) and his colleagues argue for the use of flash cards and drills with toddlers, most educators advocate a more natural approach, capitalizing upon everyday interactions parents and children have with the written word.

Part of the methodological debate stems from a particular mind-set about what it means for a person to be literate. We typically speak of a child "learning to read" around age 5 or 6. Yet, common sense tells us that for the average child, the process of becoming literate hardly occurs overnight. Children in literate societies have great exposure to, and knowledge of writing long before they learn to read. At the same time, none of us really believes that a 6-year-old "knows how to read" just because he can decipher text. (Why else do we run reading classes throughout the elementary school years and literature classes thereafter?)

In recent years, the phrase *emergent literacy* has become popular, characterizing the gradual process through which a normal middle-class child in a literate society learns to read (and then write). Building upon earlier work by Marie Clay (1972), Teale and Sulzby (1986) argue that we can better understand the process whereby children learn to read if we replace the notion of *reading readiness* with *emergent literacy*.

From Reading Readiness to Emergent Literacy

The term *reading readiness* first formally appeared in 1925 in the *Yearbook of the United States National Society for the Study of Education*. The phrase referred to the natural, *maturational* process believed to take place before children could learn to read. However, by the late 1950s and the 1960s, as intervention programs for early child development became increasingly popular (e.g., the Head Start program), *reading readiness* began referring to the *experiences* children had that were directly related to literacy.

Yet, despite this shift in emphasis, two assumptions have continued to undergird beliefs about reading readiness. The first is the belief in a sharp distinction between readiness skills and actual reading. The second is the assumption that such readiness skills can only be taught in school or in a school-like setting.

Bucking the prevailing trends, a handful of psychologists and reading specialists began to question both assumptions. In the words of Yetta Goodman (1984, p.102), "It slowly became obvious to me that children's discoveries about literacy in a literate society such as ours must begin much earlier than at school age." This alternative position looks upon eventual reading and writing skills as but one end of a literacy spectrum, whose roots begin soon after a child in a literate, middle-class community is born.

Emergent Literacy / Emergent Speech

The idea of emergent literacy is hardly esoteric. The notion encompasses any experiences the growing child has with the written word. By the end of the first year of life, children generally understand that books have fronts and backs, that they have pages to be turned, and that words accompany the stuff on those pages. By age 2, most children comprehend that print in some way represents spoken language. By age 3, children have emerging concepts of how the material between the covers is likely to be structured. Stories generally have beginnings, middles, and ends. (When Aneil was 2;6, he proclaimed "The end!" at the close of every book we read, regardless of the words printed on the final page.)

Taking literacy as a continuum, we begin to see the varied ways in which children become acquainted with reading and writing. The most obvious is by having literate companions read stories or go through picture books. But any written message can be fair game, including box tops, traffic signs, or sides of buses. Children themselves play at reading and later, as they develop sufficient manual dexterity, play at writing. Children see parents read and write, fetch the newspaper in the morning, and visit bookstores and libraries.

I vividly remember the day when Aneil, age 2;8, demanded that we go to the library. "What for?", I asked. "Readee book," he responded matter-of-factly. We happened to be on my university campus, so I happily obliged. Once inside the building, he marched straight to the National Union Catalogue, the nearest books in sight. With all his strength he drew down one of the massive volumes. Opening the front cover, he proceded to leaf through 20 or 30 pages at a time, intently scanning the text. When he reached the end, he declared "Finish," and struggled to return the book to its rightful place on the shelf.

Reflecting upon how Aneil had mastered the routine, it suddenly became obvious that emergent literacy is no different from what we might call *emergent speech*. Just as we model literacy activities long before children can make sense of what we are doing, we model speech to uncomprehending newborns. In the case of speech, adult modeling slowly elicits meaningful linguistic exchange. Single words give way to syntax. The richer the interaction, the better the head-start the child has in becoming linguistically fluent. The entire process begins at birth and takes many years. Just so with literacy: The infant's inattentiveness gives way to turn-taking and sharing (e.g., turning the pages of a picture book), interaction (e.g., identifying pictures), imitation (e.g., remembering lines from the story), and independent language production (reading or writing on one's own).

Once we look at literacy skills as emerging in much the same way as spoken language, we can begin asking how adults, in the course of normal parenting routines, can help their children become literate.

PARENTS, CHILDREN, AND BOOKS: SOME DATA
Books and Conversation
Children's earliest exposure to the written word generally comes about through joint "reading" of picture books with adults. Yet, building foundations for later literacy is hardly parents' motivation for reading to very young children. Rather, such reading structures parent-child social interaction and provides a rich opportunity to teach children about the concrete world without needing to haul dinosaurs and dalmatians, camels and cabooses into one's living room.

In the process of reading to young children, parents end up teaching a great deal of new vocabulary and conversational routines. A number of studies (e.g., Ninio & Bruner, 1978; Snow & Goldfield, 1983; Wheeler, 1983; DeLoache & DeMendoza, 1987) have explored the natural ways in which maternal reading styles (e.g., labeling items in books, asking names of pictured items, encouraging conversation about the story-line, increasing one's level of linguistic demands as the child matures) lead to children's enhanced spoken language development.

Do all parents make equal use of picture-book reading as a medium for language instruction? Of course not. We are not surprised to learn that lower-class mothers are less "instructive" during reading sessions with their children than middle-class mothers, and that middle-class children evidence larger productive vocabularies (Ninio, 1980). But, what may come as a surprise are the differences in reading habits amongst middle-class parents—and in concomitant effects on their children's spoken language abilities.

A group of researchers at SUNY Stony Brook (Whitehurst, Falco, Lonigan, Fischel, DeBaryshe, Valdez-Menchaca, & Caulfield, 1988) studied the effects of reading style in 30 families as they read to children between the ages of 21 and 35 months. Half of the children were read to normally, while parents of the other half received explicit training on how to read. Parents in the experimental group were instructed to

(1) increase the rate at which they asked open-ended questions of their children ("Tell me more about what is happening"), increase their use of function-attribute questions (e.g., "What is it doing?"), and increase the number of children's utterances they expanded (e.g., in response to her child's "Happy," the mother might comment, "Yes, the pig is very happy");

(2) respond appropriately to the child's attempt to answer questions;

(3) decrease the amount of straight reading without conversational interruption;

(4) decrease the number of questions asked that the child can answer simply by pointing.

After a month, the children's spoken language abilities were assessed. Children whose parents had been trained in the above techniques spoke longer sentences, uttered more phrases, and used fewer single words than did children in the control group. These differences were still evident six months later, although the gap between groups was less pronounced.

It is obvious that parents can use reading to expand children's spoken language skills. But what about the potential effect of parents on their children's emerging *reading* skills?

Reading to Children / Children Reading

Not surprisingly, the amount parents read to young children predicts their children's subsequent reading abilities. Wells (1985), for example, reports a correlation between the frequency with which children between the ages of 1 and 3 listened to stories and (1) their level of literacy at age 5 and (2) their reading comprehension at age 7.

But, reading storybooks is hardly the only influence parents can have on their children's emerging literacy. While storybook reading requires both a book and a relatively quiet setting, modern literate societies have countless other opportunities for enhancing literacy. Here are just a few.

(1) naming letters and numbers on found objects (e.g., single letters in sections of an auditorium; numbers on the backs of buses or at the ends of grocery store aisles)
(2) reading traffic signs (STOP, ONE WAY, YIELD) while driving
(3) reading messages on buses and trucks
(4) reading food packaging
(5) counting objects at every possible opportunity

Initially, "reading" may mean attaching a whole-word label in context. As the child learns the alphabet (which may well be by age 2), such casual reading can be preceded or followed by the child decoding each of the letters in turn (e.g., "STOP. S.T.O.P."). If parents naturally engage in this kind of reading as they move through the day, children can learn an amazing amount about deciphering letters and numbers without heavy-handed pedagogical effort.

A third avenue for fostering reading skills is emphasizing rhymes in the young child's spoken and written world. From nursery rhymes to *A Child's Garden of Verse* and Dr. Seuss books, rhyming has long been a vital part of the language heard by English-speaking children. But, besides simply providing enjoyment, rhymes are an excellent device for teaching relationships between words and sound patterns and, in the process, for helping children decompose words. *Cat* is teamed with *rat*, but they differ in initial sounds. An understanding of just these differences is a vital component of learning to read.

Not surprisingly, research has shown that preschoolers' knowledge of rhymes correlates positively with early reading skills. Maclean, Bryant, and Bradley (1987) tested a group of 66 3-year-olds for their knowledge of nursery rhymes, asking the children if they could recite "Humpty Dumpty," "Baa-Baa Black Sheep," "Hickory Dickory Dock," "Jack and Jill," and "Twinkle Twinkle Little Star." Over the next year and a half, the same children were tested on a number of typical reading-readiness tasks, including detection of rhyming words; production of rhyming words; alliteration; segmentation of utterances into words, syllables, or phonemes; recognizing letters; and reading whole words. Children who had a good knowledge of nursery rhymes at age 3 regularly scored higher on these tasks. The authors conclude that

> [n]ursery rhymes are one example of the informal way in which parents, for the most part unwittingly, draw their children's attention to the fact that words have separable component sounds. The direct practical implication of our research is that an increase in the amount of experience that 3-year-old children have with nursery rhymes should lead to a corresponding improvement in their awareness of sounds, and hence to greater success in learning to read. (p. 280)

Do As I Say, Not As I Do

Like many parents of young children, I have spent hours browsing in children's bookstores. I am ceaselessly amazed at the number and variety of people purchasing books for children. Judging from the sizable dollars spent, one might have great hopes for the literacy level of the next generation. Visits to story-reading sessions in nursery programs and public libraries only enhance this impression.

Yet, the data do not support this idyllic prediction. Leaving aside for the moment disadvantaged populations, we still see an enormous discrepancy between the excitement middle-class parents have about reading to their toddlers or preschoolers, and the attitude these same children have toward reading when they grow up. While nearly all middle-class children learn basic literacy skills, comparatively few go on to become avid readers. The bloom of early literacy generally fades.

What goes wrong? While a full explanation is hardly possible here, one critical factor is clear: Most parents are not avid readers. As George Steiner observed in "After the Book?" (1972), reading is no longer an individual activity we engage in to increase our personal knowledge or for personal enjoyment. Rather, reading has become a chore we perform for a salary. Books are things we keep in our offices, not our homes. (If you doubt the correctness of this observation, check with successful real estate agents who see the contents of hundreds of homes each year.)

What has changed our reading habits? Again the explanation is far from simple. Yet, many people *believe* they know the answer. The culprit most often cited is television. Parents worry that children spend hours glued before the set instead of reading. Teachers complain that book reports are based on television mini-series instead of on books themselves.

Is television necessarily the enemy of reading? Or can it, when properly used, actually enhance the growth of literacy?

THE VIDEO REVOLUTION

Television was introduced in 1939 when, at the New York World's Fair, President Franklin D. Roosevelt broadcast the first transmission. However, it was not until the 1950s that television began to permeate the market.

By the 1950s, parents and educators had already begun to worry about the effect television might be having upon school-aged children (e.g., Maccoby, 1951). Were children watching television instead of studying? Would television make them anti-social? Concerns about television viewing heightened in the 1960s and 1970s as the amount of violence portrayed on the screen increased dramatically. By the 1980s, not only was video violence an increasing problem (particularly with the proliferation of cable programming), but the amount of time the television was turned on had skyrocketed to an average of over 40 hours a week. Admittedly, just because the set is on does not mean people are watching it, or that they are not engaged in another activity simultaneously (see, for example, Anderson, Field, Collins, Lorch, & Nathan, 1985). But, the statistics do suggest that television has become a fundamental component of family life.

Does the medium of television truly lack redeeming social virtues? Hardly. Our experiences over the past 20 years have made clear that, properly used, television can be a superb medium of instruction, even for the very young. And among the things that can successfully be taught on television are the rudiments of reading.

THE PATIENT PEDAGOGUE

Television as an educational medium has several obvious advantages over traditional pedagogy. To begin with, television provides visualizations of experiences that parents cannot easily provide: animated versions of fairy tales, pictures of Mt. Etna erupting, film clips from World War II. But secondly, television—like the computer—never gets tired. Whereas parents grow weary of telling the same story time and again, television programming allows for repetition. With the proliferation of video cassette recorders (VCRs), the capacity for repetition becomes nearly infinite.

For young children, television often proves an ideal medium of instruction. Its images rivet the child's attention. Its message is directed exclusively to the child—no brothers or sisters, telephones or doorbells vie for the "speaker's" attention. Toddlers and preschoolers are highly observant, highly imitative, and love repetition. As a medium, television is potentially tailor-made for these needs.

Potentially. Has the potential been realized?

The Road to *Sesame Street*

The answer is a resounding "yes," and the credit goes overwhelmingly to one woman: Joan Ganz Cooney. Cooney is founder of the Children's Television Workshop—the creator of *Sesame Street*, the children's program that revolutionized our thinking about the educational potential of television.

Sesame Street grew out of a study for the Carnegie Corporation that Cooney had done in 1966 on the prospects for educational television in this country. Working closely with educators and psychologists at Harvard, the new Children's Television Workshop set about designing a television program with explicit educational goals. By 1968, the following goals were established, for example, for teaching pre-schoolers letters of the alphabet.

1. Given a set of symbols, either all letters or all numbers, the child knows whether those symbols are used in reading or in counting.
2. Given a printed letter, the child can select the identical letter from a set of printed letters.
3. Given a printed letter, the child can select its other case version from a set of printed letters.
4. Given a verbal label for certain letters, the child can select the appropriate letter from a set of printed letters.
5. Given a printed letter, the child can provide the verbal label.
6. Given a series of words presented orally, all beginning with the same letter, the child can make up another word or pick another word starting with the same letter.
7. Given a spoken letter, the child can select a set of pictures or objects beginning with that letter.
8. The child can recite the alphabet.

(G. Lesser, 1974, pp.62-63)

Comparable goals were defined for teaching numbers, geometric shapes, body parts, size relationships, and so on.

Since its inaugural program in 1969, *Sesame Street* has profoundly influenced educational patterns—and levels—of preschool children. Although the program has not been without critics (e.g., Holt, 1971; H. Lesser, 1977), educators generally agree that *Sesame Street* is singlehandedly responsible for raising the emergent literacy skills of children across this country and around the world.

Originally targeted at disadvantaged urban youngsters (hence the set design and choice of characters), the program is watched today by children from all socioeconomic backgrounds and geographic regions. And although the programming is designed for children from age 3 to 5, babies as young as 12 months watch it with rapt attention.

Learning from Television

We turn now from *Sesame Street* itself to the broader question of how much language and how many language-related skills children can learn from watching television. Because much of the critique of children's television is based on the assumption that television is a passive medium, many educators have questioned how much learning can go on with an "interlocutor" who cannot talk back.

Some early studies (e.g., Nelson, 1973) noted a negative correlation between spoken language development and the amount of time a young child (between age 1 and 2) watched television. Is there more to the story?

For those who want hard data, we point to a study by Rice and Woodsmall (1988) demonstrating that 3- and 5-year-old children learn new vocabulary items after only brief exposure to the words on television. Yet, anyone with a young child who has watched much children's television does not need formal studies to confirm that an enormous amount of language learning takes place when children watch television. Examples from my own son's experience (prior to his association with other children and adults in nursery school) include the words *puce, exit, cooperation, triangle, square,* and *angry*— none of which we used in our own language directed to Aneil before he began using the words himself.

But, learning from television hardly ends with new vocabulary. Young children learn a great deal about conversational appropriateness, conventions for storytelling, and politeness formulas from watching conversations modeled on television. Similarly, television offers modeling of complex syntax. While mothers tend to simplify and shorten the sentences they address to toddlers (see Chapter 7), children's television provides an important balance of more adult grammar. In Aneil's case, I am convinced (though I cannot prove) that his use of modal expressions (e.g., "Maybe I'll do it" or "Would you like some coffee?") originated with syntax modeled on *Sesame Street*.

Given the evidence, what do we make of earlier studies that report negative correlations between television viewing and spoken language development? The explanation probably lies in variables for which the initial studies did not control.

One of these variables is the condition under which the child watched television. Was she simply parked in front of the set to free up the parents for other activities, or did the parents spend time watching alongside the child—thereby creating a three-way "conversation"? Even the most conscientious of us have been known to use the television as a babysitter. Yet, before concluding that viewing itself is harmful, we need to know how much other time parents spend speaking with their children and modeling language directly.

A second consideration is whether or not the child is actually attending to the television image. A study by Anderson and Levin (1976) reported that at age 12 months, babies attended an average of less than 20% of the time to a black-and-white segment of *Sesame Street*, and that children younger than 30 months "did not systematically monitor the TV screen but rather had their attention 'captured' for short periods of time" (p. 810). If an infant or toddler is literally parked before a screen on which she is not focusing, we can hardly expect her to be learning. Obviously, time spent interacting with a parent would be preferable.

Third, assuming the child is attending to the video image, we need to rethink whether television viewing is really a passive activity. A welter of research (see Bryant & Anderson, 1983) has argued that our intuitive assumption that television watching is necessarily a passive activity is simply wrong in many instances, especially when children are involved. Again, my own experience in watching Aneil watch television confirms that the video medium itself in no way necessarily implies a passive viewer. I have home videos to prove that when certain favorite segments of *Sesame Street* come on, Aneil joined along in the singing, answered questions posed by favorite characters, and mimicked the actions portrayed on the screen. After such episodes, he had truly gotten both a good physical and linguistic workout.

But fourth, we need to be patient in assessing the possible influences of television viewing on language development. Many of the language skills children imbibe through viewing may not appear until months or years later in their own speech. In Aneil's case, for example, delayed phonological development coupled with a cautious pronunciation strategy made him hesitant to attempt many of the words he understood from watching *Sesame Street*. Only by trying picture recognition in a book did we realize, for example, that by age 16 months he had learned the meanings of *square, circle,* and *triangle.*

MIXING MEDIA: TELEVISION AND BOOKS
TV as Conversation
We have already alluded to the question of whether children watch television in isolation or in the company of another language user. Mabel Rice and her colleagues have argued that parents can use television as a "talking picture book" that, like hard-copy books, serves as a scaffold upon which to hang modeled linguistic structures that facilitate language acquisition (Lemish & Rice, 1986).

Citing Wells, Lemish and Rice note that the ideal environment for language learning is

> a shared activity with an adult in which the adult [gives] linguistic expression to just those meanings in the situation which the child [is] capable of intending, and to which they are at that moment paying attention.
> (Wells, 1974, p. 267)

The authors go on to point up Snow and Goldfield's observation (1983) that the two aspects of parental book-reading with children that most contribute to children's language acquisition are (1) the routinization of the book-reading situation and (2) the predictability of the adult's language (Lemish & Rice, 1986, p. 252).

Television can offer precisely these conditions. Like children's books, children's television is designed in self-contained episodes with familiar characters who provide opportunities for questions and answers. Over time, these episodes become familiar and predictable. Much as with his favorite stories, Aneil had favorite segments of *Sesame Street*. His interaction with these special books and video segments was remarkably similar. In both cases, he anticipated events, vocally followed along with the narrative (i.e., verbally shadowing me as I read or the character as it spoke on television), and threw in a lot of body English when the episode got really exciting.

In fact, Aneil had so taken television as a form of conversation that when I was not physically present where he was watching, he still included me as a member of the conversational group. Among his repertoire of video favorites between age 2 and 3 were several episodes in which trains or airplanes appeared. About 30 seconds before the train or plane was due on the screen, Aneil would come tearing into the kitchen yelling "Train!" (or "Airplane!"), grab my hand, and literally drag me into the living room in time to share in the transportation scene.

TV Viewing and Reading Revisited

Finally, let us return to the question that continues to worry parents who find their preschoolers absorbed in television: Doesn't television viewing negatively correlate with reading ability? If so, whatever the early language benefits of television, shouldn't we be worried that we are spawning illiterate television junkies?

A number of studies (e.g., Ridder, 1963; Hornik, 1978; Morgan, 1980) have reported a negative correlation between reading ability (and school achievement more generally) and the amount of television watching done by junior high school children. Yet, when we scratch beneath the surface, we find the story is really more complex.

One obvious question is whether such negative correlations result from failing to control for variables like intelligence, socioeconomic status, and parental education. It is now fairly clear (e.g., Zuckermann, Singer, & Singer, 1980; Hornik, 1981; Neuman, 1980) that among bright children from educated, economically sound households, there is no negative correlation between reading ability and television viewing.

Another variable to examine is the amount of viewing itself. Like a fine red wine that must age (but not too much), some television viewing (but not too much) *positively* correlates with reading abilities. Williams, Haertel, Haertel, and Walberg (1982) found that reading achievement improved slightly for children who watched television up to 10 hours a week, and Anderson, Wilson, and Fielding (1988) note positive correlations for fifth graders who viewed television up to 20 hours weekly. Similarly, the National Assessment of Educational Progress (NAEP) study done in 1979-1980 (National Assessment of Educational Progress, 1981) found the highest reading scores amongst 9-year-olds who watched three to four hours of television daily. In all three studies, amounts of television viewing higher than these correlated negatively with reading scores.

Age itself turns out to be a relevant variable in assessing possible effects of television viewing on reading abilities. The NAEP survey just mentioned found positive correlations between reading performance and television watching for 9-year-olds but negative correlations between the variables for 13- and 17-year-olds (the three age groups tested).

And what about very young children—those below the age of 5? Does early television viewing help or hinder the acquisition of literacy skills? A proper experiment for addressing this question is obviously out of the question. Besides needing to control for hours of viewing, we would need to control for subject matter viewed, amount and type of picture-book reading, and even content of adult-child conversation. Who would want to be in the control group deprived of picture books or of *Sesame Street*?

We can, however, make some inferences from observational data. In a study of 11 children who were reading before the age of 4, Salzer (1984) reports that in most cases, "the child had learned [to read] independently, largely as a result of watching SESAME STREET," and that some of the children had begun to watch fairly regularly before the age of 1 (p. 95). In several instances, children watched the program up to 2 or 3 hours a day.

Interestingly, other studies (e.g., Patel & Patterson, 1982) suggest that while early spoken language development may correlate positively with intelligence, early reading ability does not seem to correlate either with intelligence or with general spoken language development. Instead, the strong correlation for early reading is with family attitude, particularly with maternal views on the importance of education, emotional support, and cognitive stimulation. Given that good children's educational television programming provides strong components of this support, it is reasonable to conclude that properly used, early television watching can be a boon to subsequent literacy.

9

Problems Illusory and Elusive

IS MY CHILD NORMAL?

The process of raising a child can be a harrowing experience. Parents tend to worry at every turn. Stories that fill the daily newspaper ("I just turned my back for a second . . . ") press us into constant vigilance.

Also troubling are the times we are not sure there *is* a problem. Such uncertainty often arises when assessing children's linguistic development. Is the child linguistically on track? Is the problem you think you detect transitory or really serious? What should you be doing to help?

In this chapter, we will talk about how parents can spot difficulties, compensate and nurture as needed, or, where appropriate, seek professional guidance. We will also look at illusory problems that children outgrow or that were never really problems at all. (See Bishop & Mogford, 1988, for an in-depth discussion of many of the issued raised in this chapter.)

BIRTH ISSUES
Prematurity

Six weeks before my son was due, he was born.

We were very fortunate. Although Aneil was early, he was healthy—all five pounds of him. What special care would he need? Would he grow up physically and cognitively intact? How long would it take for him to catch up with children born at term? The physicians assured me he would develop normally. (I reminded myself that both Sir Isaac Newton and Winston Churchill were born prematurely.) But, on the question of how long it would take to catch up—and what, if anything, I might do to help, neither the neonatologist, the intensive care staff, nor the pediatrician had any information to offer.

Nearly 10% of babies born in the United States today are premature (defined as more than three weeks early). A sizable number of those are born to healthy middle-class mothers who took their vitamins, foreswore alcohol and cigarettes, and exercised religiously. Obviously, premature children with other complications might be expected to have language problems (see, for example, Tolkin-Eppel, 1984; Hubatch, Johnson, Kistler, Burns, & Moneka, 1985). But what about "normal" (i.e., low risk) preemies?

The literature on this group is sparse. Holmqvist, Regefalk, and Svenningsen (1987) report that at 9 months of age, the premature babies in their study linguistically lagged behind a full-term control group. (NOTE: In studies comparing premature children with full-term infants, it is standard practice to "correct" for prematurity by calculating age from when the baby was due, not when the baby was born.) At age 9 months, while 80% of the control group spoke between one and three words, fewer than 10% of the premature children had any recognizable words. As 4-year-olds, the differences had begun to even out, although the premature children born at younger than 33 weeks of gestation still had shorter syntactic combinations. Moreover, by age 4, nearly twice as many premature children had been diagnosed as having speech disorders. Largo, Molinari, Pinto, Weber, and Duc (1986) report similar results, noting moderate language delays up through age 5 among the children born prematurely.

What explains this initial language delay? In some cases, inadequate control over the vocal apparatus is at least partly responsible. The production of speech sounds is a complex neural activity, even for wholly normal babies—a single sound may take up to 35 or more muscles to articulate (Hardcastle, 1976). Consider Aneil. As an infant, he had cooed and gurgled normally during the first 3 months of life. But as for babbling, he was almost a nonstarter. In fact, the boy did most of his babbling between the ages of 1 and 2 (rather than during the normal period from 6 months to 1 year). Up until almost age 2;6, Aneil did little spontaneous vocalizing. Moreover, before 2;6, Aneil had no real syntax, and all of his words were monosyllabic. Once the articulatory apparatus was under control, Aneil's word length and expressive syntax exploded. By age 2;11 he was using 10 and 11 word sentences and correctly pronouncing such words as *fantastic, helicopter,* and *tomorrow.*

Moving from physiological to social explanations, to what extent does language delay in premature children result from parental presuppositions and social responses? In a study of social interaction between mothers and their 3- and 5-month-babies, Lester, Hoffman, and Brazelton (1985) discovered differential mothering patterns depending upon whether the child had been born at term or was premature. The researchers were interested in how mother and infant "responded" to each other: Who took the lead in the interaction? Did the mother follow up on behaviors the child initiated, or did she initiate a new action instead? Results clearly showed that while the term infants dominated the interaction by age 3 months (and more so at 5 months), the pre-term babies showed no such dominance at either age. Noting that mothers of pre-term infants often remark upon how difficult it is to understand and anticipate their baby's behavior, the authors conclude that the premature infant's difficulty in establishing early communicative interaction may contribute to eventual language delay.

A curious question, of course, is how much of that poor early interaction results from neurological immaturity in processing environmental input, and how much is actually *caused* by the parents themselves. We know (e.g., Condry & Condry, 1976; Hildebrandt & Fitzgerald, 1979) that adults react differently to infants that are identified as girls or boys, regardless of the baby's actual sex. Does the label "premature" also engender special behaviors or attitudes? Stern and Hildebrandt (1984) discovered that when shown videotapes of 9-month-old infants, their subjects (including college undergraduates and mothers of 3- to 18-month-old infants) judged the children who had been labeled "premature" as being smaller, less attentive, slower, less smart, more sleepy, and more passive than infants who had been labeled "full term."

The implications of Stern and Hildebrandt's findings are profound. Parents with premature babies are likely to perceive their children as physically, socially, cognitively, and behaviorally immature, whether or not such is actually the case. Many parents are less likely to vocalize to children who themselves do not vocalize much. Yet, the linguistic prognosis for premature children is deeply tied to the amount of interaction that parents initiate. It is, therefore, exceedingly important that parents of children born prematurely overcompensate for understandable tendencies to draw back linguistically and socially.

Multiple Births

In Chapter 4, we spoke about the time demands that twins (or triplets) place upon parents. What does the literature say about the linguistic prognosis for children who typically must compete for linguistic attention?

A long line of twin studies (e.g., Day, 1932; Mittler, 1970; Tomasello, Mannle, & Kruger, 1986; Alin-Åkerman, 1987; Hay, Prior, Collett, & Williams, 1987) have reported that twins lag behind singletons in language development. These differences are often pronounced up through at least age 3 or 4. Twins generally vocalize less as infants, are later in using first words, have poorer articulation, and are slower to develop syntactically. By age 5 or 6, most of these differences have disappeared, although some studies (e.g., Johnston, Prior, & Hay, 1984) indicate that twins—especially boys—are more likely to encounter reading problems in school.

Most researchers agree (e.g., Lytton, Conway, & Sauvé, 1977; Tomasello et al., 1986) that the cause of delay is overwhelmingly the truncated linguistic interaction with each twin, not a biological problem. Parents are advised to work consciously at spending individual time with each twin (as opposed to addressing the two collectively) and not to worry unduly. Past experience proves that twins do, indeed, catch up.

Birth Order

Twins are the extreme example of siblings born within a few years of each other. The same constraints on parental attention apply: Parents cannot linguistically interact as much with two or more young children as they can with a single child.

It is hardly surprising, then, that data on language acquisition rates among younger born children closely resemble those of twins. All other factors being equal, younger siblings are slower to develop linguistically than first-borns (e.g., McCarthy, 1954; Nelson, 1973). (NOTE: This finding must be balanced with an understanding that girls, generally speaking, are faster in their early language development than boys). As in the case of twins, there is no cause for alarm. Many of us are living proof that younger children acquire quite sophisticated linguistic abilities and are none the worse for having developed their language a few months later than their older brothers or sisters.

THE BILINGUAL QUESTION

The most common question I am asked about language by foreign students and colleagues is whether they should raise their children bilingually. The query has an odd ring, because the people inquiring are themselves bilingual. However, given contemporary attitudes toward bilingualism in America—from the precarious status of Title VII school bilingual education programs to the current movement spearheaded by S. I. Hayakawa to make English our official language (e.g., Hayakawa, 1987), these concerns are understandable. (See the March 1988 issue of *English Journal* for a balanced summary of the issues.)

My answer stems from three considerations: linguistic, educational, and pragmatic. Linguistically, learning two languages as a child is hardly exceptional. Millions of people do it naturally and well (see Grosjean, 1982). As long as both languages are adequately and consistently modeled in the home and/or in the community, any healthy child can grow up bilingually. (See, e.g., Harding & Riley, 1986, for an overview of the issues in raising a bilingual child.)

Educationally, bilingualism has two concrete advantages. Besides the obvious fact that bilingual individuals can function in two languages (and generally in two cultures), there is evidence (e.g., Lambert & Anisfeld, 1969; Diaz, 1983) that the demands of handling more than one language system may favorably affect some dimensions of cognitive functioning. The current debate over bilingual education in America is more a dispute over social policy than over the linguistic issue of whether children can thrive educationally in a bilingual setting (see Hakuta, 1986).

But finally, we need to include practical considerations. A family of uneducated immigrants at the far end of the social spectrum might understandably encourage their children's English at the expense of the family's mother tongue. A doctoral student from Germany might not hesitate to raise her son bilingually while she studies in America.

Often the child's personal attitudes or peer group pressures help settle the issue. Children may simply rebel against using a language not spoken by their peers. Yet, a determined parent can often prevail against unfavorable odds. A colleague of mine, the daughter of Russian immigrants, recounts how throughout her childhood she resented her parents for making her speak Russian at home. Growing up during the height of the Cold War, she felt enormous social pressures to drop her Slavic heritage. As an adult, though, she is grateful for the opportunity to live bilingually and biculturally.

GROWING PAINS

It is only natural that interested parents keep a close eye on their developing child's language and express concern if something seems amiss. Even being a professional linguist does not alleviate concern over potential problems. David Crystal, an authority on both language acquisition and language disorders, describes his personal uneasiness when his toddler son went through a period of stuttering (Crystal, 1986). Crystal's professional sense told him the stuttering would pass, but meanwhile he worried as much as any other parent.

Slow To Talk

Parents' most common concern is that their children are slow in beginning to talk. On average, children utter their first words somewhere around age 12 months, have a spoken vocabulary of about 50 words by age 18 months, and begin to combine words by age 2. The "normal" variation around these averages is enormous: Many children speak a first recognizable word by 9 months while other perfectly healthy children do not do so until nearly 18 months. The same diversity exists for syntax. Whereas some children combine words by their first birthday, others (who will soon become linguistically indistinguishable from the syntactic early birds) are pushing age 3 before uttering novel two-word utterances.

Parental anxiety has two sources. On the one hand, parents want to be sure nothing is actually wrong with their children. On the other hand, children with only minimal vocabulary and syntax render meaningful communication extremely difficult. Admittedly, infants of 5 or 6 months also have very little productive language, but they have limited needs as well. A change of diaper, offer of food, or human company solves most problems. With toddlers, the number of intended meanings can be immense—as can the problems deriving from lack of parental understanding.

Why are some children slower to speak than others? We do not really know. Relatively benign causes of delay include slower neurological development, shy temperament, or presence of other siblings. More serious possibilities are hearing disorders or elusive problems such as childhood aphasia (see below).

When should parents begin to worry? If you have not heard a first intelligible word by age 2 or signs of syntactic combinations by age 3, consultations with professionals (hearing specialists, speech therapists) are definitely in order. Before then, the biggest linguistic boost parents can give children is to keep talking and listening, providing as rich a language environment as possible.

I Can't Understand You

If children who are slow linguistic starters prove frustrating for parents, children with unintelligible speech can be exasperating. Besides struggling to decipher a child's meaning, parents are concerned that failure on their part to comprehend will lead the child to stop trying to use language to communicate.

In reading most of the literature on normal language acquisition, one might conclude that unintelligible pronunciation is a rare problem in young children. That illusion comes from the fact that, until relatively recently, language acquisition specialists intentionally chose as their subjects children whose language they could understand. One can hardly blame them. It turns out, though, that clear articulators often approach language learning from a different angle than children with articulation problems. While clear articulators tend to work on one word at a time, many children with initial articulation difficulties are actually attempting entire phrases or sentences, and only gradually do they render comprehensible the pieces of the whole.

Aneil was one of the garblers. He would say, "See grz duh," and from the context I would venture, "Yes, look at the cars, Daddy." Inevitably, he would start to scream in desperation. Only later would I realize he had actually been saying, "See the garage over there." (I was unaware he even knew the words *garage* and *there*.) Suggestions? Have patience, work hard at deciphering the code, and, when in doubt, try circumlocution (e.g., "Yes, indeed, I see it too!"). Asking a struggling child for clarification is sometimes appropriate, but oftentimes it leads a child to withdraw in frustration.

Stuttering

A third parental nightmare is stuttering. Most of us have known people who stutter, and we are pained to imagine our children going through life unable to begin sentences without tremendous physical effort and psychological stress.

While some children never outgrow stuttering, most do. As we noted a moment ago, a transitory period of stuttering is common among children (especially boys) somewhere around age 2 or 3. What causes this stuttering? It is hard to know for certain, though early stuttering may come about because of an overload on the cognitive system. Many children begin to stutter as their syntactic abilities grow. Aneil, for example, entered a serious period of stuttering between the ages of 2;6 and 2;8. It was also at this time that he made the transition from monosyllabic to polysyllabic words, and from single words to syntax.

Another cause of stuttering is stress: an illness or death in the family, divorce, or the arrival of a new sibling. Webster (1988) notes that in a British study of the language of children up through age 5,

> [a] history of speech dysfluency (stammer or stutter) was reported in 6% of children and significantly associated with young maternal age, substitute parenthood, large numbers of young siblings, and traumatic events such as frequent house moves. (p. 87)

When he was 2;9—and just coming out of his earlier stuttering, Aneil switched nursery schools. His first day at the new school, Aneil was nearly silent. His second day, the silence by day was coupled with severe stuttering at night. By the end of the third day, the child was struggling with every utterance. I prepared to remove him from the school immediately. Thankfully, a calmer head prevailed. The nursery director gently reminded me that children in new surroundings typically pass through a period of readjustment, and that the stuttering would pass. Indeed it did. By the fifth day, Aneil's articulation was back to normal.

Stuttering can also be brought on by well-intentioned or good-humored conversation. A speech therapist tells the story of innocently correcting her 3-year-old's grammar several times, and the girl's sliding into months of stuttering. A relative recounts how a cousin used to tease his babysitter by mocking the unfortunate girl's stuttering. The mocking led to a habit, and to this day, the cousin (now in his 40s) still stutters.

The best strategy for parents of preschoolers who are episodic stutterers is to do nothing: Do not react to the stuttering, do not comment upon it. Simply continue to model good, clear language. If stress seems to be the cause, provide extra loving and understanding until the trauma passes.

More serious, persistent cases of stuttering should be referred to speech therapists. For the stuttering itself is only half of a growing child's problem. The other—and equally worrisome—half is the teasing the child is likely to endure from playmates.

INTANGIBLES: APHASIA, DELAY, DISABILITY

The most infuriating language problems are those that seem to have no name. An otherwise happy, healthy, intelligent child does not appear to be making satisfactory linguistic progress—a 3-year-old with a 10-word vocabulary or a 4-year-old who puts only two words together. Something is obviously wrong, but what?

Therapists label such children *developmental* (or *childhood*) *aphasics*, *language-disabled*, or *specific-language-impaired* (see Lahey, 1988). In all probability, these problems have a neurological explanation. Whatever the cause, speech therapy—and lots of patience—are in order. Often children seem to "outgrow" their delay problems. Much as you may not know whether your headache would have disappeared without the aspirin, it is hard to ascertain if therapy for these children "worked," or if the children simply matured.

CLASSIC PROBLEMS: SENSORY, NEUROLOGICAL, COGNITIVE, PSYCHOLOGICAL

The last class of problems is comprised of the ones with names, diagnoses, and prognoses. They include language difficulties caused by sensory deficits (especially deafness), neurological problems (particularly cerebral palsy), cognitive deficits (i.e., mental retardation), and psychological disorders (notably autism). All of these difficulties require sound professional help.

The good news is that the possibilities for normal language development, at least in the cases of deafness and cerebral palsy, are impressive. A tremendous amount of hard work—from both parent and child—is entailed, but the efforts can pay off. The prognosis for language development among children who are retarded or autistic is less good, although experiments with alternative language systems (including versions of American Sign Language) have shown some promise (e.g., Bricker, 1972; Bonvillian & Nelson, 1976).

The sensory deficit of blindness poses a particularly interesting linguistic challenge. The auditory and vocal apparatus are intact, but the visual medium through which we form so many of our real-world experiences is missing. As many of us know from personal acqaintances, blind people can and do develop spoken language skills comparable to those of their sighted counterparts. Several studies (e.g., Andersen, Dunlea, & Kekelis, 1984; Landau & Gleitman, 1985) have documented how that process takes place. But, as in the case of deaf children or children with cerebral palsy, the struggle toward normalcy is aided by constant linguistic modeling from the parents, teachers, or therapists.

One final sensory difficulty is minor hearing loss or recurrent ear infections (see Klein & Rapin, 1988). Parents are far more likely to encounter these than deafness or blindness, retardation or autism. Auditory amplification for children with mild hearing losses can enable children to develop language normally. Careful attention to possible ear infections may help prevent hearing loss in the first place.

10

Conclusions and Challenges

What is the role of parents in children's language learning? In the preceding chapters, we have explored the symbiotic relationship between children's inherent creativity and personality on the one hand, and parental modeling and socialization on the other. As a result, we have a growing sense of the critical input of adults in the language development/acquisition/learning process.

To summarize what we have learned, we can lay out some essential linguistic advice to parents of young children.

* Keep talking to infants and toddlers, even if they are unable to answer back.
* Treat children as conversational partners, listening to and building upon what they say (even if it is incomplete—or incoherent).
* Follow as well as lead in conversation (and when leading, ask open-ended questions where appropriate).
* Don't worry about using a baby talk register. Such transient usage does not retard children's linguistic development, and it often helps in expressing affect, building social interaction, and even teaching language.
* With several young children in the same household, give each your exclusive attention as often as possible.
* Weave pedagogy naturally into conversation.
* Have patience during times of linguistic start-up and transition.

Amongst the lessons we have learned in this book, one of the most important is to realize how little we know. Challenges for future study of the role of parents in language acquisition include the following questions.

* In seeking correlations between adult usage and children's linguistic development, which linguistic constructions do we choose to study?
* How do we move from noting correlations between children's and parents' language to providing causal explanations?
* What effect do the age and education level of parents have upon their use of baby talk features in addressing young children?
* What are the differential and complementary roles of contemporary fathers and mothers in children's language development?
* How does the language adults address to children alter as children become older and increasingly linguistic?
* What effect does television have upon children's developing vocabulary, syntax, and literacy?
* How can we use what we have learned about linguistic interaction in middle-class households to assist in the linguistic development of disadvantaged or disabled populations?

Yet, perhaps our biggest challenge is to puzzle out what to do with the growing amounts of data and the number of explanations we obtain. In more whimsical moments, I conjure up visions of parents carrying around plastic-coated conversational crib sheets saying things like, "Beware of test questions" or "Use short sentences until the child develops syntax, and then switch to long sentences." Mercifully, these moments pass quickly and are replaced with the common-sensical realization that, at least as of now, we have no evidence to establish that specific adult linguistic patterns have a lasting effect upon children's eventual mastery of language.

In closing, we might do well to bear in mind a lesson taught me by a nurse discussing how to administer CPR to a young child. Those who have been through CPR training know that the American Red

Cross has established a specific sequence of moves to follow: positioning the victim, opening the airway, giving two breaths, checking the pulse, and so forth. Yet, few of us—even those trained in CPR—adhere to the precise sequence in actual emergencies. As the nurse observed, many an adult has saved a child by coupling basic understanding of the procedure with common sense.

The details of parents' effects on children's language—and the explanations behind them—still remain opaque. However, building upon the basic outline we have thus far, parents can benefit their progeny by following the simple logic of speaking and listening with patience, interest, and direction.

References

Ackerman-Ross, S. A. (1985). *The relationship of day care to middle-class 3-year-olds' language performance.* Unpublished doctoral dissertation, Memphis State University.

Ackerman-Ross, S. A., & Khanna, P. (1989). The relationship of high quality day care to middle-class 3-year-olds' language performance. *Early childhood research quarterly, 4*, 97-116.

Alin-Akerman, B. (1987). The expectation and parentage of twins: A study of the language development of twin infants. *Acta Geneticae Medicae et Gemellologiae, 36*, 225-232.

Andersen, E., Dunlea, A., & Kekelis, L. (1984). Blind children's language: Resolving some differences. *Journal of Child Language, 11*, 645-664.

Anderson, D., Alwitt, L., Lorch, E., & Levin, S. (1979). Watching children watch television. In G. Hale & M. Lewis (Eds.), *Attention and cognitive development* (pp. 331-361). New York: Plenum.

Anderson, D., & Levin, S. (1976). Young children's attention to "Sesame Street." *Child Development, 47*, 806-811.

Anderson, R. C., Wilson, P. T., & Fielding, L. G. (1988). Growth in reading and how children spend their time outside of school. *Reading Research Quarterly, 23*, 285-303.

Anderson, D. R., Field, D. E., Collins, P. A., Lorch, E. P., Nathan, J. G. (1985). Estimates of young children's time with television. *Child Development, 56*, 1345-1357.

Ariès, P. (1962). *Centuries of childhood: A social history of family life* (R. Baldick, Trans.). New York: Knopf.

Baker, N. D., & Nelson, K. E. (1984). Recasting and related conversational techniques for triggering syntactic advances by young children. *First Language, 5,* 3-22.

Barnes, S., Gutfreund, M., Satterly, D., & Wells, G. (1983). Characteristics of adult speech which predict children's language development. *Journal of Child Language, 10,* 65-84.

Barnett, R. C., & Baruch, G. K. (1978). *The complete woman.* New York: Irvington.

Baron, N. S. (1977). *Language acquisition and historical change.* Amsterdam: North-Holland.

Baron, N. S. (1981). *Speech, writing, and sign.* Bloomington: Indiana University Press.

Bellinger, D., & Gleason, J. B. (1982). Sex differences in parental directives to young children. *Sex Roles, 8,* 1123-1139.

Belsky, J., & Steinberg, L. D. (1978). The effects of day care: A critical review. *Child Development, 49,* 929-949.

Bishop, D., & Mogford, K. (Eds.). (1988). *Language development in exceptional circumstances.* Edinburgh: Churchill Livingstone.

Blewitt, P. (1983). Dog versus collie: Vocabulary in speech to young children. *Developmental Psychology, 19,* 602-609.

Bloom, K., Russell, A., & Wassenberg, K. (1987). Turn taking affects the quality of infant vocalizations. *Journal of Child Language, 14,* 211-227.

Bloom, L., Hood, L., & Lightbrown, P. (1974). Imitation in language development: If, when, and why. *Cognitive Psychology, 6,* 380-420.

Bloomfield, L. (1933). *Language.* New York: Holt, Rinehart, and Winston.

Blount, B. G., & Padgug, E. (1977). Prosodic, paralinguistic, & interactional features in parental speech. *Journal of Child Language, 4,* 67-86.

Bogoyavlenskiy, D. N. (1973). The acquisition of Russian inflections (G. Slobin, Trans. and D. I. Slobin, Ed.). In C. A. Ferguson & D. I. Slobin (Eds.), *Studies of child language development.* New York: Holt, Rinehart, and Winston.

Bonvillian, J., & Nelson, K. (1976). Sign language acquisition in a mute autistic boy. *Journal of Speech and Hearing Disorders, 41,* 339-347.

Bricker, D. D. (1972). Imitative sign training as a facilitator of word-object association with low-functioning children. *American*

Journal of Mental Deficiency, 76, 509-516.

Brown, R. (1958). How shall a thing be called? *Psychological Review, 65,* 14-21.

Brown, R. (1973). *A first language.* Cambridge, MA: Harvard University Press.

Brown, R., & Hanlon, C. (1970). Derivational complexity and order of acquisition in child speech. In J. R. Hayes (Ed.), *Cognition and the development of language.* New York: John Wiley.

Bryant, J., & Anderson, D. R. (Eds.). (1983). *Children's understanding of television: Research on attention and comprehension.* New York: Academic Press.

Bühler, K. (1934). *Sprachtheorie.* Jena: Gustav Fischer.

Buss, A. H., & Plomin, R. (1984). *Temperament: Early developing personality traits.* Hillsdale, NJ: Erlbaum.

Cameron, J., Livson, N. & Bayley, N. (1967, July 21). Infant vocalizations and their relationship to mature intelligence. *Science,* 331-333.

Caporael, L. R., & Culbertson, G. H. (1986). Verbal response modes of baby talk and other speech at institutions for the aged. *Language and Communication, 6,* 99-112.

Cazden, D. (1965). *Environmental assistance to the child's acquisition of grammar.* Unpublished doctoral dissertation, Harvard University.

Cherry, L., & Lewis, M. (1976). Mothers and two-year-olds: A story of sex-differentiated aspects of verbal interaction. *Developmental Psychology, 12,* 278-282.

Chomsky, N. (1959). Review of *Verbal Behavior* by B. F. Skinner. *Language, 35,* 26-58.

Chomsky, N. (1965). *Aspects of the theory of syntax.* Cambridge, MA: MIT Press.

Clark, R. (1977). What's the use of imitation? *Journal of Child Language, 4,* 341-358.

Clay, M. (1972). *Reading: The patterning of complex behavior.* Auckland: Heinemann Educational.

Cochran, M. M. (1977). A comparison of group day and family child-rearing patterns in Sweden. *Child Development,, 48,* 702-707.

Condry, J., & Condry, S. (1976). Sex differences: A study of the eye of the beholder. *Child Development, 47,* 812-819.

Conway, D., Lytton, H., & Pysh, F. (1980). Twin-singleton language differences. *Canadian Journal of Behavioral Science, 12,* 264-271.

Cross, T. G. (1977). Mothers' speech adjustments: The contributions of selected child listener variables. In C. E. Snow & C. A. Ferguson (Eds.), *Talking to children: Language input and acquisition.* Cambridge: Cambridge University Press.

Cross, T. G. (1978). Mothers' speech and its association with linguistic development in young children. In N. Waterson & C. E. Snow (Eds.), *The development of communication.* New York: Wiley.

Crystal, D. (1986). *Listen to your child.* Penguin: New York.

Davis, E. (1937). The development of linguistic skill in twins, singletons with siblings, and only children from age five to ten years. *University of Minnesota Institute of Child Welfare Monograph, 14.*

Day, E. (1932). The development of language in twins: A comparison of twins and single children. *Child Development, 3,* 179-199.

Della Corte, M., Benedict, H., & Klein, D. (1983). The relationship of pragmatic dimensions to the referential-expressive distinction. *Journal of Child Language, 10,* 35-44.

DeLoache, J. S., & DeMendoza, O. A. P. (1987). Joint picturebook interactions of mothers and 1-year-old children. *British Journal of Developmental Psychology, 15,* 111-123.

de Mause, L. (Ed.). (1975). *The history of childhood.* New York: Harper and Row.

Demetras, M. J., Post, K. N., & Snow, C. E. (1986). Feedback to first language learners: The role of repetitions and clarification questions. *Journal of Child Language, 13,* 275-292.

Devereux, G. (1949). Mohave voice and speech mannerisms. *Word, 5,* 268-272.

Diaz, R. (1983). Thought and two languages: The impact of bilingualism on cognitive development. In E. Norbeck, D. Price-Williams, & W. McCord (Eds.), *Review of Research in Education* (Vol. 10). Washington, DC: American Educational Research Association.

Doman, G. (1963). *How to teach your baby to read: The gentle revolution.* New York: Random House.

Dunn, J., & Kendrick, C. (1982). The speech of two- and three-year-olds to infant siblings: "Baby talk" and the context of communication. *Journal of Child Language, 9,* 579-595.

Elbers, L., & Ton, J. (1985). Play pen monologues: The interplay of words and babbles in the first words period. *Journal of Child Language, 12,* 551-565.

Ervin-Tripp, S., & Miller, W. (1977). Early discourse: Some questions about questions. In M. Lewis & L. A. Rosenblum (Eds.), *Interaction, conversation, and the development of language.* New York: Wiley.

Ferguson, C. A. (1964). Baby talk in six languages. *American Anthropologist 66*(6, pt. 2), 103-114.

Fernald, A. (1985). Four-month-old infants prefer to listen to motherese. *Infant Behavior and Development, 8,* 181-195.

Fernald, A., & Kuhl, P. (1987). Acoustic determinants of infant preference for motherese speech. *Infant Behavior and Development, 10,* 279-293.

Fernald, A., & Simon, T. (1984). Expanded intonation contours in mothers' speech to newborns. *Developmental Psychology, 20,* 104-113.

Furrow, D., & Nelson, K. (1984). Environmental correlates of individual differences in language acquisition. *Journal of Child Language, 11,* 523-534.

Furrow, D., & Nelson, K. (1986). A further look at the motherese hypothesis: A reply to Gleitman, Newport, & Gleitman. *Journal of Child Language, 13,* 163-176.

Furrow, D., Nelson, K., & Benedict, H. (1979). Mothers' speech to children and syntactic development: Some simple relationships. *Journal of Child Language, 6,* 423-442.

Garnica, O. (1977). Some prosodic and paralinguistic features of speech to young children. In C. E. Snow & C. A. Ferguson (Eds.), *Talking to children: Language input and acquisition.* Cambridge: Cambridge University Press.

Gleason, J. B. (1987). Sex differences in parent-child interaction. In S. Stede & C. Tanz (Eds.), *Language, gender, and sex in contemporary perspective.* Cambridge: Cambridge University Press.

Gleitman, L. R., Newport, E. L., & Gleitman, H. (1984). The current status of the motherese hypothesis. *Journal of Child Language, 11,* 43-79.

Goldberg, S., & Lewis, M. (1969). Play behaviors in the year old infant: Early sex differences. *Child Development, 40,* 21-31.

Golinkoff, R. M., & Ames, G. J. (1979). A comparison of fathers' and mothers' speech with their young children. *Child Development*, *50*, 28-32.

Goodman, Y. M. (1984). The development of initial literacy. In H. Goelman, A. Oberg, & F. Smith (Eds.), *Awakening to literacy*. Exeter, NH: Heinemann Educational.

Greif, E. B. (1980). Sex differences in parent-child conversation. *Women's Studies International Quarterly*, *3*, 253-258.

Grieser, D. L., & Kuhl, P. (1988). Maternal speech to infants in a tonal language: Support for universal prosodic features in motherese. *Developmental Psychology*, *24*, 14-20.

Grosjean, F. (1982). *Life with two languages*. Cambridge, MA: Harvard University Press.

Hanson, N. R. (1958). *Patterns of discovery*. Cambridge: Cambridge University Press.

Hakuta, K. (1986). *The mirror of language*. New York: Basic Books.

Hardcastle, W. J. (1976). *Physiology of speech*. New York: Academic Press.

Harding, E., & Riley, P. (1986). *The bilingual family: A handbook for parents*. New York: Cambridge University Press.

Hardy-Brown, K., & Plomin, R. (1985). Infant communicative development: Evidence from adoptive and biological families for genetic and environmental influences on rate differences. *Developmental Psychology*, *21*, 378-385.

Hay, D. A., Prior, M., Collett, S., & Williams, M. (1987). Speech and language development in preschool twins. *Acta Geneticae Medicae et Gemellologiae*, *36*, 213-223.

Hayakawa, S. I. (1987). Make English official: One common language makes our nation work. *The Executive Educator*, *9*, 36+.

Hildebrandt, K., & Fitzgerald, H. (1979). Adults' perceptions of infant sex and cuteness. *Sex Roles*, *5*, 471-481.

Hirsh-Pasek, K., & Treiman, R. (1982). Doggerel: Motherese in a new context. *Journal of Child Language*, *9*, 229-237.

Hirsh-Pasek, K., Treiman, R., & Schneiderman, M. (1984). Brown & Hanlon revisited: Mothers' sensitivity to ungrammatical forms. *Journal of Child Language*, *11*, 81-88.

Hladik, E. G., & Edwards, H. T. (1984). A comparative analysis of mother-father speech in the naturalistic home environment. *Journal of Psycholinguistic Research*, *13*, 321-332.

Hoff-Ginsberg, E. (1985). Some contributions of mothers' speech to their children's syntactic growth. *Journal of Child Language, 12,* 367-385.

Hoff-Ginsberg, E. (1986). Function and structure in maternal speech: Their relation to the child's development of syntax. *Developmental Psychology, 22,* 155-163.

Hoff-Ginsberg, E. (1987). Why some properties of maternal speech benefit language growth (and others do not). Paper presented at meetings of the Society for Research in Child Development, Baltimore, MD.

Hoff-Ginsberg, E., & Shatz, M. (1982). Linguistic input and the child's acquisition of language. *Psychological Bulletin, 92,* 3-26.

Holmqvist, P., Regefalk, C., & Svenningsen, N. W. (1987). Low risk vaginally born preterm infants: A four year psychological and neurodevelopmental follow-up study. *Journal of Perinatal Medicine, 15,* 61-72.

Holt, J. (1971, May). Big Bird, meet Dick and Jane. *Atlantic Monthly.*

Hornik, R. C. (1978). Television access and the slowing of cognitive growth. *American Educational Research Journal, 15,* 1-15.

Hornik, R. C. (1981). Out-of-school television and schooling: Hypotheses and methods. *Review of Educational Research, 51,* 193-214.

Hubatch, L. M., Johnson, C. J., Kistler, D. J., Burns, W. J., & Moneka, W. (1985). Early language abilities of high-risk infants. *Journal of Speech and Hearing Disorders, 50,* 195-207.

Hummel, D. D. (1982). Syntactic and conversational characteristics in fathers' speech. *Journal of Psycholinguistic Research, 11,* 465-483.

Hymes, D. (1974). *Foundations in sociolinguistics.* Philadelphia: University of Pennsylvania Press.

Inhelder, B., & Piaget, J. (1969). *The early growth of logic in the child.* New York: W.W. Norton.

Jakobson, R. (1960). Closing statement: Linguistics and poetics. In T. A. Sebeok (Ed.), *Style in Language.* Cambridge, MA: MIT Press.

Jakobson, R. (1968). *Child language, aphasia, and phonological universals* (A.R. Keiler, Trans.). The Hague: Mouton.

Johnston, C., Prior, M., & Hay, D. (1984). Prediction of reading disability in twin boys. *Developmental Medicine and Child Neurology, 26,* 588-595.

Jones, C. P., & Adamson, L. B. (1987). Language use in mother-child and mother-child-sibling interactions. *Child Development, 58,* 356-366.

Kavanaugh, R. D., & Jirkovsky, A. M. (1982). Parental speech to young children: A longitudinal analysis. *Merrill-Palmer Quarterly, 28,* 297-311.

Klein, S. K., & Rapin, I. (1988). Intermittent conductive hearing loss and language development. In D. Bishop & K. Mogford (Eds.), *Language development in exceptional circumstances.* Edinburgh: Churchill Livingstone.

Lahey, M. (1988). *Language disorders and language development.* New York: Macmillan.

Landau, B., & Gleitman, L. R. (1985). *Language and experience: Evidence from the blind child.* Cambridge, MA: Harvard University Press.

Lambert, W. E., & Anisfeld, E. (1969). A note on the relationship of bilingualism and intelligence. *Canadian Journal of Behavioral Science, 1,* 123-128.

Largo, R. H., Molinari, L., Pinto, L. Comenale, Weber, M., & Duc, G. (1986). Language development of term and preterm children during the first five years of life. *Developmental Medicine and Child Neurology, 28,* 333-350.

Leiderman, P. H., Tulkin, S. R., & Rosenfeld, A. (Eds.). (1977). *Culture and infancy: Variations in the human experience.* New York: Academic Press.

Lemish, D., & Rice, M. L. (1986). Television as a talking picture book: A prop for language acquisition. *Journal of Child Language, 13,* 251-274.

Leonard, L. B., Chapman, K., Rowan, L. E., & Weiss, A. L. (1983). Three hypotheses concerning young children's imitation of lexical items. *Developmental Psychology, 19,* 591-601.

Leopold, W. (1939-1949). *Speech development of a bilingual child* (4 vols.). Evanston: Northwestern University Press.

Lesser, G. S. (1974). *Children and television: Lessons from Sesame Street.* New York: Random House.

Lesser, H. (1977). *Television and the preschool child.* New York: Academic Press.

Lester, B. M., Hoffman, J., & Brazelton, T. B. (1985). Interaction in term and preterm infants. *Child Development, 56,* 15-27.

Lewis, M. (1957). *How children learn to speak.* London: George G. Harrap.

Lewis, M. (1969). Infants' responses to facial stimuli during the first year of life. *Developmental Psychology, 1,* 75-86.

Lewis, M., & Feiring, C. (1982). Some American families at dinner. In L. M. Laosa & I. E. Sigel (Eds.), *Families as learning environments for children.* New York: Plenum.

Lewis, M., & Freedle, R.O. (1973). Mother-infant dyad: The cradle of meaning. In P. Pilner, L. Kramer, & T. Alloway (Eds.), *Communication and affect: Language and thought.* New York: Academic Press.

Lieven, E. V. M. (1978). Conversations between mothers and young children: Individual differences and their possible implications for the study of language learning. In N. Waterson & C. E. Snow (Eds.), *The development of communication.* New York: Wiley.

Lieven, E. V. M. (1984). Interactional style and children's language learning. *Topics in language disorders,* 15-23.

Lyons, J. (1971). *Introduction to theoretical linguistics.* Cambridge: Cambridge University Press.

Lytton, H., Conway, D., & Suavé, R. (1977). The impact of twinship on parent-child interaction. *Journal of personality and social psychology, 35,* 97-107.

Maccoby, E. E. (1951). Television: Its impact on school children. *Public Opinion Quarterly, 15,* 421-444.

Maccoby, E. E., & Jacklin, C. N. (1974). *The Psychology of Sex Differences.* Stanford: Stanford University Press.

Maclean, M., Bryant, P., & Bradley, L. (1987). Rhymes, nursery rhymes, and reading in early childhood. *Merrill-Palmer Quarterly, 33,* 255-281.

Malone, M. J., & Guy, R. F. (1982). A comparison of mothers' and fathers' speech to their 3-year-old sons. *Journal of Psycholinguistic Research, 11,* 599-608.

Malraux, A. (1949-1950). *The Psychology of Art* (S. Gilbert, Trans.). New York: Pantheon.

McCarthy, D. (1954). Language development in children. In L. Carmichael (Ed.), *Manual of Child Psychology* (2nd ed.). New York: John Wiley & Sons.

McCartney, K. (1984). Effects of quality day care environment on children's language development. *Developmental Psychology, 20,* 244-260.

McDonald, L. O. (1979). *A functional analysis of individual differences in conversational style among mothers.* Unpublished doctoral dissertation, University of Oregon.

McDonald, L., & Pien, D. (1982). Mother conversational behavior as a function of interactional intent. *Journal of Child Language, 9,* 337-358.

McLaughlin, B., White, D., McDevitt, T., & Raskin, R. (1983). Mothers' and fathers' speech to their young children: Similar or different? *Journal of Child Language, 10,* 245-252.

Masur, E., & Gleason, J. S. (1980). Parent-child interaction and the acquisition of lexical information during play. *Developmental Psychology, 16,* 404-409.

Mehler, J., Bertoncini, J., Barrière, M., & Jassik-Gerschenfeld, D. 1978. Infant recognition of mother's voice. *Perception, 7,* 491-497.

Mervis, C.B., & Mervis, C.A. (1982). Leopards are kitty-cats: Object labeling by mothers for their thirteen-month-olds. *Child Development, 53,* 267-273.

Mittler, P. (1970). Biological and social aspects of language development in twins. *Developmental Medicine and Child Neurology, 12,* 741-757.

Moerk, E. L. (1972). Principles of interaction in language learning. *Merrill-Palmer Quarterly, 18,* 229-257.

Moerk, E. L. (1980). Relationships between parental input frequencies and children's language acquisition: A reanalysis of Brown's data. *Journal of Child Language, 7,* 105-118.

Morgan, M. (1980). Television viewing and reading: Does more equal better? *Journal of Communication, 30,* 159-165.

Moss, H. (1967). Sex, age, and state as determinants of mother-infant interaction. *Merrill-Palmer Quarterly, 13,* 19-36.

Munroe, R. H., Munroe, R. L., & Whiting, B. B. (Eds.). (1981). *Handbook of cross-cultural human development.* New York: Garland.

Murry, L., & Trevarthen, C. (1986). The infant's role in mother-infant communication. *Journal of Child Language, 13,* 15-29.

National Assessment of Educational Progress. (1981). *Procedural handbook: 1979-80 reading and literature assessment.* Denver:

Education Commission of the States.

Nelson, K. (1973). Structure and strategy in learning to talk. *Monographs of the Society for Research in Child Development, 38* (1-2, Serial No. 149).

Nelson, K. (1981). Individual differences in language development: Implications for development and language. *Developmental Psychology, 16,* 170-187.

Nelson, K. (Ed.). 1989. *Narratives from the crib.* Cambridge, MA: Harvard University Press.

Nelson, K. E. (1977). Facilitating children's syntax acquisition. *Developmental Psychology, 13,* 101-107.

Nelson, K. E., Baker, N. D., Denninger, M., Bonvillian, J. D., & Kaplan, B. J. (1985). *Cookie* versus *do-it-again*: Imitative-referential and personal-social-syntactic-initiating language styles in young children. *Linguistics, 23,* 433-454.

Nelson, K. E., Carskaddon, G., & Bonvillian, J. D. (1973). Syntax acquisition: Impact of experimental variation in adult verbal interaction with the child. *Child Development, 44,* 497-504.

Nelson, K. E., Denninger, M. M., Bonvillian, J. D., Kaplan, B. J., & Baker, N. D. (1984). Maternal input adjustments and non-adjustments as related to children's linguistic advances and to language acquisition theories. In A. D. Pellegrini & T. S. Yawkey (Eds.), *The development of oral and written language: Readings in developmental and applied linguistics.* New York: Ablex.

Nelson, K. E., Denninger, M., Kaplan, B., & Bonvillian, J. D. (1979). Varied angles on how children progress in syntax. Paper presented at the meetings of the Society for Research in Child Development, San Francisco.

Neuman, S. B. (1980). Television: Its effects on reading and school achievement. *The Reading Teacher, 33,* 801-805.

Newport, E. L., Gleitman, H., & Gleitman, L. R. (1977). Mother, I'd rather do it myself: Some effects and non-effects of maternal speech style. In C. E. Snow & C. A. Ferguson (Eds.), *Talking to children: Language input and acquisition.* Cambridge: Cambridge University Press.

Ninio, A. (1980). Picture-book reading in mother-infant dyads belonging to two sub-groups in Israel. *Child Development, 51,* 587-590.

Ninio, A., & Bruner, J. (1978). The achievement and antecedents of labelling. *Journal of Child Language, 5*, 1-15.

Ninio, A., & Rinott, N. (1988). Fathers' involvement in the care of their infants and their attributions of cognitive competence to infants. *Child Development, 59*, 652-663.

O'Brien, M., & Nagle, K. (1987). Parents' speech to toddlers: The effect of play context. *Journal of Child Language, 14*, 269-279.

Ochs, E. (1982). Talking to children in Western Samoa. *Language and Society, 11*, 77-104.

Oller, D. K. (1981). Infant vocalizations: Exploration and reflexivity. In R. Stark (Ed.), *Language behavior in infancy and early childhood*. New York: Elsevier.

Olsen-Fulero, L. (1982). Style and stability in mother conversational behavior: A study of individual differences. *Journal of Child Language, 9*, 543-564.

Patel, P. G., & Patterson, P. (1982). Precocious reading acquisition: Psycholinguistic development, IQ, and home background. *First Language, 3*, 139-153.

Penner, S. G. (1987). Parental responses to grammatical and ungrammatical child utterances. *Child Development, 58*, 376-384.

Pezdek, K., Lehrer, A., & Simon, S. (1984). The relationship between reading and cognitive processing of television and radio. *Child Development, 55*, 2072-2082.

Pollock, L. A. (1983). *Forgotten children: Parent-child relations from 1500 to 1900*. Cambridge: Cambridge University Press.

Popova, M. I. (1973). Grammatical elements of language in the speech of pre-school children (G. Slobin, Trans. and D. I. Slobin, Ed.). In C. A. Ferguson & D. I. Slobin (Eds.), *Studies of child language development*. New York: Holt, Rinehart, and Winston.

Pye, C. (1986). Quiche Mayan speech to children. *Journal of Child Language, 13*, 85-100.

Ratner, N. B. (1988). Patterns of parental vocabulary selections in speech to very young children. *Journal of Child Language, 15*, 481-492.

Ratner, N. B., & Pye, C. (1984). Higher pitch in baby talk is not universal: Acoustic evidence from Quiché Mayan. *Journal of Child Language, 11*, 515-522.

Remick, H. (1976). Maternal speech to children during language acquisition. In W. von Raffler-Engel & Y. Lebrun (Eds.), *Baby talk and infant speech*. Amsterdam: Swets & Zeitlinger.

Retherford, K. S., Schwartz, B. C., & Chapman, R. S. (1981). Semantic roles and residual grammatical categories in mother and child speech: Who tunes into whom? *Journal of Child Language, 8*, 583-608.

Rice, M. L., & Woodsmall, L. (1988). Lessons from television: Children's word learning when viewing. *Child Development, 59*, 420-429.

Ridder, J. M. (1963). Pupil opinion and the relationship of television to academic achievement. *Journal of Educational Research, 57*, 204-206.

Roe, K., Drivas, A., Karagellis, A., & Roe, A. (1985). Sex differences in vocal interaction with mother and stranger in Greek infants: Some cognitive implications. *Developmental Psychology, 21*, 372-377.

Rondal, J. A. (1980). Fathers' and mothers' speech in early language development. *Journal of Child Language, 7*, 353-369.

Rosch, E. H., Mervis, C. B., Gary, W., Johnson, D., & Boyes-Braem, P. (1976). Basic objects in natural categories. *Cognitive Psychology, 8*, 382-439.

Roth, F. P. (1984). Accelerating language learning in young children. *Journal of Child Language, 11*, 89-107.

Salzer, R. T. (1984). Early reading and giftedness: Some observations and questions. *Gifted Child Quarterly, 28*, 95-96.

Savic, S. (1980). *How twins learn to talk*. New York: Academic Press.

Schieffelin, B. (1979). Getting it together: An ethnographic approach to the study of the development of communicative competence. In E. Ochs & B. Schieffelin (Eds.), *Developmental pragmatics*. New York: Academic Press.

Schwartz, R. G., Chapman, K., Prelock, P. A., Terrell, B., & Rowan, L. E. (1985). Facilitation of early syntax through discourse structure. *Journal of Child Language, 12*, 13-25.

Skinner, B. F. (1957). *Verbal behavior*. New York: Appleton-Century-Crofts.

Slobin, D. I. (1973). Cognitive prerequisites for the development of grammar. In C. A. Ferguson & D. I. Slobin (Eds.), *Studies of child language development*. New York: Holt, Rinehart, & Winston.

Smolak, L. (1987). Child characteristics and maternal speech. *Journal of Child Language, 14,* 481-492.

Smolak, L., & Weinraub, M. (1983). Maternal speech: Strategy or response? *Journal of Child Language, 10,* 369-380.

Snow, C. E. (1972). Mothers' speech to children learning language. *Child Development, 43,* 549-565.

Snow, C. E. (1977). The development of conversation between mothers and babies. *Journal of Child Language, 7,* 1-22.

Snow, C. E. (1978). The uses of imitation. *Journal of Child Language, 8,* 205-212.

Snow, C. E. (1986). Conversations with children. In P. Fletcher & M. Garman (Eds.), *Language acquisition* (2nd ed.). Cambridge: Cambridge University Press.

Snow, C. E., & Ferguson, C. A. (Eds.). (1977). *Talking to children: Language input and acquisition.* Cambridge: Cambridge University Press.

Snow, C. E., & Goldfield, B. A. (1983). Turn the page please: Situation-specific language acquisition. *Journal of Child Language, 10,* 551-569.

Speidel, G. E. (1987). Conversation and language learning in the classroom. In K. E. Nelson (Ed.), *Children's language* (Vol. 6). Hillsdale, NJ: Erlbaum.

Speidel, G. E., & Nelson, K. E. (Eds.). (1989). *The many faces of imitation in language learning.* New York: Springer-Verlag.

Steiner, G. (1972). After the book? *Visible Language, 6,* 197-210.

Stern, D. N., Spieker, S., Barnett, R. K., & MacKain, K. (1983). The prosody of maternal speech: Infant age and context related changes. *Journal of Child Language, 10,* 1-15.

Stern, M. & Hildebrandt, K. A. (1984). Prematurity stereotype: Effects of labeling on adults' perceptions of infants. *Developmental Psychology, 20,* 360-362.

Sturm, H., & Jorg, S. (1981). *Information processing by young children: Piaget's theory applied to radio and television.* Munich: K.G. Saur.

Teale, W. H., and Sulzby, E. (Eds.). (1986). *Emergent literacy: Writing and reading.* Norwood, NJ: Ablex.

Thomas, A., & Chess, S. (1977). *Temperament and development.* New York: Brunner/Mazel.

Tolkin-Eppel, P. S. (1984). *Language development in premature and high risk children*. Unpublished doctoral dissertation, McMaster University, Ontario, Canada.

Tomasello, M., Mannle, S., & Kruger, A. C. (1986). Linguistic environment of 1- and 2-year-old twins. *Developmental Psychology, 22,* 169-176.

Triandis, H.C., & Heron, A. (Eds.). (1981). *Handbook of cross-cultural psychology (Vol. 4: Developmental psychology).* Boston: Allyn & Bacon.

U.S. Department of Labor (Aug., 1989). *Handbook of labor statistics.* Bureau of Labor Statistics. Bulletin # 2340. Washington, DC: U.S. Government Printing Office.

Vihman, M. M., Macken, M. A., Miller, R., Simmons, H., & Miller, J. (1985). From babbling to speech: A re-assessment of the continuity issue. *Language, 61,* 397-445.

Webster, A. (1988). The prevalence of speech and language difficulties in childhood: Some brief research notes. *Child Language Teaching and Therapy, 4,* 85-91.

Weintraub, S. (1977). Parents' speech to children: Some situational and sex differences. Paper presented to the New England Psychological Association, Worcester, MA.

Weitzman, N., Birns, B., & Friend, R. (1985). Traditional and nontraditional mothers' communication with their daughters and sons. *Child Development, 56,* 894-898.

Wellen, C.J. (1985). Effects of older siblings on the language young children hear and produce. *Journal of Speech and Hearing Disorders, 50,* 84-99.

Wells, G. (1974). Learning to code experience through language. *Journal of Child Language, 1,* 243-269.

Wells, G. (1980). Adjustments in adult-child conversation: Some effects of interaction. In H. Giles, W. P. Robinson, & P. M. Smith (Eds.), *Language: Social psychological perspectives.* Oxford: Pergamon.

Wells, G. (1984). *Language development in the preschool years.* Cambridge: Cambridge University Press.

Wells, G. (1985). Preschool literacy-related activities and success in school. In D. R. Olson, N. Torrance, & A. Hildyard (Eds.), *Literacy, language, and learning.* Cambridge: Cambridge University Press.

Wells, G. (1986). Variation in child language. In P. Fletcher & M. Garman (Eds.), *Language acquisition* (2nd ed.). Cambridge: Cambridge University Press.

Wertsch, J. V. (1985). *Vygotsky and the social formation of mind*. Cambridge, MA: Harvard University Press.

Wheeler, M. P. (1983). Context-related age changes in mothers' speech: Joint book reading. *Journal of Child Language, 10*, 259-263.

Williams, P. A., Haertel, E. H., Haertel, G. D., & Walberg, H. J. (1982). The impact of leisure-time television on school learning: A research synthesis. *American Educational Research Journal, 19*, 19-50.

Whitehurst, G. J., Falco, F. L., Lonigan, C. J., Fischel, J. E., DeBaryshe, B. D., Valdez-Menchaca, M. C., & Caulfield, M. (1988). Accelerating language development through picture book reading. *Developmental Psychology, 24*, 552-559.

Woollett, A. (1986). The influence of older siblings on the language environment of young children. *British Journal of Developmental Psychology, 4*, 235-245.

Yoder, P. J., & Kaiser, A. P. (1989). Alternative explanations for the relationship between maternal verbal interaction style and child language development. *Journal of Child Language, 16*, 141-160.

Zuckermann, D. M., Singer, D. G., & Singer, J. L. (1980). Television viewing, children's reading, and related classroom behavior. *Journal of Communication, 30*, 166-174.

About the Author

Naomi S. Baron (Ph.D. in linguistics, Stanford University) is currently a professor of linguistics in the Department of Language and Foreign Studies at The American University, Washington, DC. There, she is also Associate Dean of the College of Arts and Sciences. Dr. Baron has taught classes on child language acquisition for over 15 years and published many articles in the fields of linguistics, semiotics, computers, and education. Her most recent books are *Computer Languages: A Guide for the Perplexed*, Doubleday; and *Speech, Writing and Sign*, Indiana University Press.